SERVING God with DETERMINED faith

Studies in the Book of Nehemiah

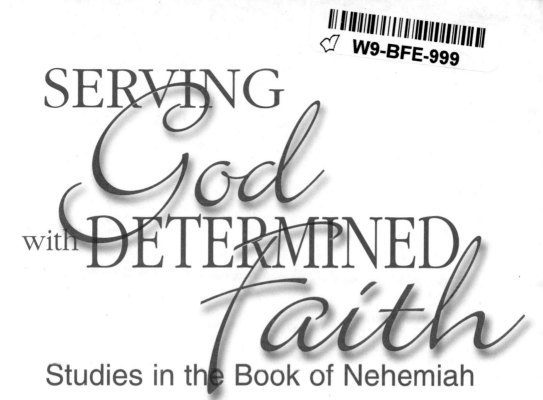

Written by

BRUCE WARE

Adult January Bible Study 2006
LifeWay Press®
Nashville, TN

ISBN: 0-6330-9959-1

This book is a resource in the Leadership and Skill Development category of the Christian Growth Study Plan.
Course CG-1123

Subject Area: Bible Studies
Dewey Decimal Classification Number: 222.8
Subject Heading: BIBLE. O.T. NEHEMIAH \ DISCIPLESHIP \ FAITH

Printed in the United States of America.

Leadership and Adult Publishing
LifeWay Church Resources
One LifeWay Plaza
Nashville, TN 37234-0175

We believe the Bible has God for its author; salvation for its end; and truth, without any mixture of error, for its matter and that all Scripture is totally true and trustworthy. The 2000 statement of *The Baptist Faith and Message* is our doctrinal guideline.

Cover Image: Corbis/clipart.com

SERVING God with DETERMINED Faith

From the Editor. 4
Christian Growth Study Plan 96

Session 1

Respond Courageously to Spiritual Challenges (Neh. 1:1–3:32)

Chapter 1   Looking to God for Help (Neh. 1:1-11) 5
Chapter 2   Taking Steps of Faith (Neh. 2:1-8,11-18; 3:1-5). 18

Session 2

Stay Focused on God's Work (Neh. 4:1–7:73a)

Chapter 3   Overcoming Obstacles (Neh. 4:6-23; 5:1-13). 31
Chapter 4   Finishing God's Work (Neh. 6:1-19; 7:1-5a,66-73a) 44

Session 3

Renew Your Relationship with God (Neh. 7:73b–10:39)

Chapter 5   Renewing Your Worship (Neh. 7:73b–8:18). 57
Chapter 6   Renewing the Covenant Community (Neh. 9:1–10:39) . . 70

Session 4

Seek Opportunities to Serve (Neh. 11:1–13:31)

Chapter 7   Willing and Determined to Serve 83
             (Neh. 11:1-18; 12:27-43; 13:6-31)

From the Editor

The Book of Nehemiah begins with an enormous challenge that Nehemiah could have received with despair but instead he received with prayer. Nehemiah's character is displayed not only through this initial incident but throughout the book. Nehemiah was a man of faith, humility, and deep dependence on God. He recognized that God alone was his hope for the task that lay before him. On the other hand, Nehemiah was a man of courage, determination, and valor. He did not passively wait for God to act but actively undertook to accomplish God's plan. Other men of faith (such as Ezra) also demonstrated their determination to serve God despite the difficulties they faced. This study is designed to help adults understand that biblical faith involves dependent, humble faith and courageous, determined valor.

This **Learner Guide** for **January Bible Study 2006** is designed to help adults understand God's message in the Book of Nehemiah and apply that message to their lives. It is written in an informal, easy-to-read style and explains the biblical text without extensive comments. This Learner Guide has several aids to enhance your study of the Book of Nehemiah. These helps include:

- Two **learning activities** in each chapter. Each activity is integral to the teaching plans found in the Leader Guide.
- Sets of questions (**For Your Consideration**) occur throughout each chapter. The questions can be used in individual or group study, and they can help an adult probe further after reading the Scripture and related textbook material. Both the questions and the learning activities can help a leader generate discussion.
- At least one feature entitled **A Closer Look** in each chapter, which elaborates on or provides summary information on related chapter topics.

At the beginning of each lesson you will find the **Bible Truth** and the **Life Impact.** The **Bible Truth** briefly states the main abiding spiritual principle *for that lesson.* The **Life Impact** identifies how learners will give evidence of spiritual transformation on an ongoing basis, so this is the main application we hope learners will take with them *after the lesson is over.*

Dr. Bruce Ware wrote the lessons for this issue of January Bible Study. Dr. Ware is professor of Christian theology and senior associate dean in the School of Theology at The Southern Baptist Theological Seminary in Louisville, Kentucky, where he has taught for seven years. Bruce is also a council member for the Council on Biblical Manhood and Womanhood and is editor of CBMW's semi annual journal. He and Jodi, his wife of 27 years, have two daughters, Bethany and Rachel.

Chapter One

Looking to God for Help

Bible Truth: *When faced with spiritual challenges, God's people can confidently look to God for guidance.*

Life Impact: *To help you look to God for guidance*

Setting the Stage

Deep dependence and unwavering determination. Reliant trust and relentless travail. Enduring confidence and engaging courage. These are the overall characteristics that shine forth through Nehemiah's life and labor. In this oft-neglected Old Testament book, we find a story of an incredible faith in God that expresses itself in a determined valor. In the face of enormous challenges and opposition, Nehemiah placed his full faith and hope in God. Yet this was no mere passive, inactive faith. Rather, Nehemiah's trust was coupled with a persevering and courageous toil to accomplish the very things for which he trusted God.

How easy it is for any of us to miss this necessary balance. Some of us have learned the need to trust God, to cast our cares and burdens on Him. But often we fail to ask *How may God want to involve me in working out the answers to my concerns?* Others of us are prone to action. We're the get-it-done type. Yet if our work does not flow from wonder at the greatness of God and from depending on His strength and wisdom, we can fail to accomplish the purposes of God—despite the earnestness of our efforts. One of the keys to serving God as we ought is found in the example of Nehemiah. Courageous and determined labor for God must flow out of heartfelt, dependent faith in God. One without the other falls short of God's design for us.

As the Book of Nehemiah begins, some Jewish exiles were still living in Babylon in the middle of the fifth century B.C. In 586 B.C., about 140

Learning Activity

Necessary Balance

Nehemiah balanced his strong faith in God with a willingness to take action himself. In the first two paragraphs of this lesson (pp. 5-6), find words and phrases that show Nehemiah's commitment to faith and his commitment to works. List the words and phrases in the appropriate column. The first two in each column have been provided to help you get started.

FAITH	WORKS
Deep dependence	*Unwavering determination*
Reliant trust	*Relentless travail*

Learning Activity

Just the Facts

Dig into Nehemiah 1:1-4 and get these basic facts to set the stage for your study of this book.

Who? (v. 1) _____

When? (v. 1) _____

Where? (v. 1) _____

What? (v. 3-4) _____

Why? (vv. 2-3) _____

years earlier, the Babylonians had conquered the Southern Kingdom of Judah (the Northern Kingdom of Israel had been taken captive by the Assyrians in 722 B.C.). Most of the Jews living in Jerusalem were taken to Babylon. Their exile in Babylon lasted until God moved Cyrus to issue a decree (538 B.C.) that the temple in Jerusalem be rebuilt. Many years earlier God had promised that He would raise up Cyrus for this purpose (see Isa. 44:28 and Jer. 25:12). The temple was finished in 516 B.C., and worship of the Lord was marvelously restored, as the Book of Ezra explains. Ezra 1:1-4 records the beginning of the promise of the temple's restoration through Cyrus's decree—70 years after the exile began. But not all faithful Jews moved back to

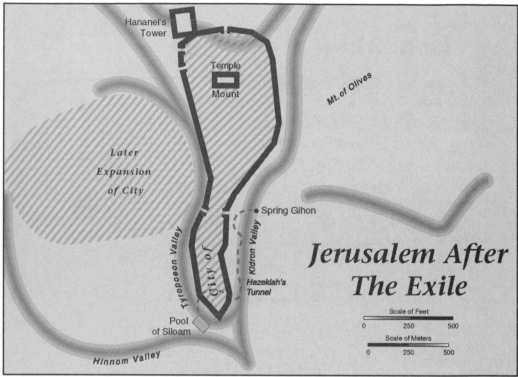

Israel at that time. Nehemiah was among those still living in Susa, the capital city of Babylon, when he received word that the walls of the city of Jerusalem were still in ruins and its inhabitants were deeply distressed (Neh. 1:3). This sets the stage, then, for the story of Nehemiah's determined faith. And what a story it is!

For Your Consideration

1. A great hymn of the faith rightly says, "Trust and obey for there's no other way." Which might be your tendency, to trust without obeying as you should, or to obey (do what is right) without a heart of trust? Why is this the case?

2. God fulfilled His word! He promised that Cyrus—who wasn't even born when Isaiah predicted this—would order the rebuilding of the temple and that it would happen 70 years after the exile. Both occurred exactly as God said. What responses in our hearts should this produce? What difference should this make in how we live?

A CLOSER LOOK

Susa

The Book of Nehemiah begins with our hero "in the fortress city of Susa" (1:1) where he served as cupbearer (v. 11) to King Artaxerxes of Persia (2:1). Where was Susa and where is it now?

Susa was the winter capital of the Persian Empire. It was located in what is now Iran, not far from the Persian Gulf. The map on page 8 shows the path that Nehemiah probably traveled from Susa to Jerusalem.

In addition to being the starting point of Nehemiah's journey, the citadel or palace in Susa played a significant role in two other Old Testament books: Esther and Daniel.

In Susa, Esther was taken into King Ahasuerus's harem. While there, she made her heroic stand on behalf of her Jewish kinsmen, and the Jewish people were able to kill their enemies who had plotted to destroy them (Esth. 1:2; 2:2-3,8-9; 9:5-6).

One of Daniel's visions was located in Susa. In that vision Daniel saw himself "in the fortress city of Susa . . . beside the Ulai Canal" (Dan. 8:2). The ram in the vision represents the Medo-Persian Empire (v. 20).

God's People in Trouble
(Neh. 1:1-3)

One of the most difficult of all human experiences is learning news of something deeply distressing or tragic. It could come from a doctor who says you have a serious illness. A phone call in the night could awaken you with news of a loved one's death. A good friend may be having marital problems. Let's face it. None of us ever wants this sort of news, and hearing it often causes deep sadness and even depression.

In the opening verses of our book, Nehemiah was confronted with disturbing news. Upon the arrival of some Jewish travelers from Judah, Nehemiah inquired about how the people of God were doing in Judah and about the city of Jerusalem itself. This was when they told Nehemiah news that must have been painful for him to hear. They said, The survivors in the province, who returned from the exile, are in great trouble and disgrace. Jerusalem's wall has been broken down, and its gates have been burned down (v. 3).

Let's think for a few minutes of the significance that this opening account has for the whole book. A few observations are needed. First, this account introduces us to the main figure of the book, a faithful Jewish believer named Nehemiah. We know nothing about this man except what we learn of him in this book. He was not a previously recognized leader of the people. He must not have had famous ancestors since his lineage is not listed at the opening of the book. Instead, all we learn of him is that he is Nehemiah, the son of Hacaliah, and that his brother Hanani was among those who traveled from Judah to Susa. Since nothing is known about Hacaliah, Nehemiah's father, it seems that the only real reason for mentioning this fact is that it distinguishes the main figure of the book from another "Nehemiah" mentioned later, the son of Azbuk (3:16).

The point is simply this: The hero of the story was a normal, faithful, prayerful, God-fearing man. Nehemiah was also an exile in Persia, the empire that joined with Media to overthrow Babylon in 538 B.C. Until this challenge came to him, he had not made a name for himself, nor was he in the line of famous people. Rather, Nehemiah was faithful to God who presented before him a great challenge. This challenging situation changed Nehemiah's life, but he exercised faith in God and stepped out in ways he had never done before. Faithfulness in the little things, Jesus explained, often brings from the Lord opportunities for faithfulness in bigger things (Matt. 25:23). This man Nehemiah, a seemingly normal yet faithful Jew who honored the Lord with his life, was given such an opportunity.

Second, only from the perspective of the whole book (and the end of the story in particular) can we talk about the news brought to Nehemiah as an opportunity. No doubt, Nehemiah did not feel this way when he was told the distressing news that moved him to prayer. But if we read the whole story and then look back at how it all began, we realize in retrospect that the distressing news Nehemiah received was in fact an opportunity to see God work in great and marvelous ways.

There is a great lesson here for all of us. Often when we receive bad news, we do not and cannot see in this news the way God has worked in it. We see only the heartache, the misery, the disappointment, and the difficulties. But the story of Nehemiah instructs us that even in the bad news there may be an opportunity from God for us to watch Him work. In the hardship we are called to trust God, to seek how He may use us, and to watch Him bring great glory to His name and wondrous good to His people—even as the result of pain and tragedy. In the bad news that God's faithful people receive, the eyes of faith will be on the lookout for the glorious purposes of God that may transform our current misery into majesty.

Third, we must not overlook just how bad this news was to Nehemiah. Centuries earlier God had chosen Jerusalem as the city where He would make His name to dwell. God's choice goes all the way back to when He called Abraham to sacrifice his son Isaac at Mount Moriah and then provided a substitute so Isaac would not have to die (Gen. 22). Mount Moriah was the future site of the city of Jerusalem. This is the city where God instructed David to build his royal residence and gave him the plans for the temple that David's son, Solomon, built. Jerusalem was the place where sacrifice for sins and worship of the true and living God were centered. Jerusalem stood for the honor of the Lord, the God of Israel, and it stood as the place of true worship and praise. Thus, for Nehemiah to hear that the wall of Jerusalem was still broken down and its gates burned was to realize that Jerusalem stood unprotected from thieves, pagan religious influences, further destruction, and idolatry. God's name still was being dishonored. Furthermore, the future of the true worship of the Lord and the blessing of God's people were in peril. For Nehemiah this was distressing news beyond his worst fears. So how did he respond? What should we do when we face distressing news?

For Your Consideration

1. What encouragement can you take from the fact that the enormous assignment God gave Nehemiah was to a normal, faithful, God-fearing person in exile in Persia? Many people think that if they are not well known or well connected, they cannot be used by God. How should Nehemiah's story help all of God's people think differently about those whom God uses to serve Him?

2. Do you have any past experiences of tragedy or distress where you, like Nehemiah, can look back and see how God intended good to come through the pain and difficulty? How can this help you face deeply distressing news? How should a Christian's response to distressing news be different from how the non-Christian would respond to the same distressing news?

3. Are you tempted to make distressing news worse or better than it really is? Some people immediately think of the worst possible situation

when they hear some distressing news; others try to ignore it and pretend it doesn't exist. What can we learn from Nehemiah about how we should receive the distressing news that comes to us?

Confession of Sin (Neh. 1:4-7)

Clearly, one of the most important lessons in the Book of Nehemiah is found in observing how Nehemiah responded to the tragic news he heard about Jerusalem. But before we look at this, notice some things he did not do. First, Nehemiah did not blame God for the condition of Jerusalem, its walls, or its gates. Second, he did not conclude that God was incapable of doing anything about it. Third, Nehemiah did not give up in despair, doubting that God was willing to deal with this horrible problem. Fourth, he did not take matters into his own hands and try to figure out how he could fix the situation on his own. None of these would be responses of faith, would they? So what did Nehemiah do in this situation?

Basically, Nehemiah responded to the distressing news he received by praying to God. Upon hearing this devastating news, he gave himself to thoughtful, prayerful consideration of what he had learned. At first, Nehemiah sat down and wept. Then for days he mourned, while also fasting and praying. During these days, surely Nehemiah must have been asking the question, *Is God saying something to me and my peo-*

ple through the broken wall and burned gates of Jerusalem? Is there a reason things are as bad as they are?

Nehemiah realized there was a reason behind this distress, that God had a purpose and a plan for it. The people of Israel had sinned against the Lord, and the broken wall of Jerusalem was a symbol of the broken relationship between God and His people. There was only one thing to do—pray to God. Nehemiah decided to uphold God's rightful lordship over all things and His covenant-keeping faithfulness toward His people. He also would confess the sins of the people of Judah and plead with God for merciful deliverance.

Nehemiah's prayer began where prayers ought to begin—with a recognition of the greatness and goodness of God. He is the LORD God of heaven and He keeps His gracious covenant with His own people. Nehemiah remembered that God had made it clear He would bless His people for their obedience and curse them when they turned from His ways. Clearly, the blessing of God was not currently resting on Jerusalem, with its broken wall and people in distress. Therefore, it must be the case that the Israelites needed to confess their sins and repent. Nehemiah acknowledged his own sinfulness as well: "Both I and my father's house have sinned."

Notice several features of Nehemiah's prayer of repentance in verses 6-7. First, his was a persistent prayer, in which he brought confessions and petitions before the Lord "day and night" on behalf of his countrymen. Second, Nehemiah's confession was corporate in nature, confessing both the sins of the people along with his own sins. There was no self-righteousness here. Third, his confession made no excuses or rationalizations. It admitted fully and honestly the condition of Israel's relationship with God. Here are marks of real confession as God sees it: lasting realization of wrongdoing, absence of self-righteousness or of one's own goodness, and an admission of wrongdoing that is devoid of excuses. With such a repentant attitude of heart, Nehemiah was now ready to bring his heart's petition before the Lord.

For Your Consideration

1. Nehemiah rightly concluded from the broken wall of Jerusalem that sin needed to be dealt with. Is this true of every trial a Christian experiences? Are some distresses of life due to sin while others come

despite our faithfulness? How can believers tell the difference?

2. Consider the three marks of Nehemiah's confession of sin. Have you had experiences in your life when these also marked your own heart before God? If these characteristics are absent, what should be concluded about a person's "confession"? What may promote moving one to have this same attitude of heart that Nehemiah had?

3. Nehemiah extolled the greatness and majesty of God, as well as His goodness and care for His people. What happens to our view of God if one "side" of these two truths of God overshadows the other? If God is great in our eyes but not good, what view of God will this leave us with? How will we live before this God? But if God is good but not great, what view of God and what sort of life follows?

Plea for God's Help (Neh. 1:8-11)

How do you turn repentance of a failed past into positive action toward the future? The way Nehemiah did this was by appealing to God to act. Nehemiah realized that the only hope he had was for God to hear and answer his prayer, and so he pleaded with God to do what God alone can do: bring the victory!

The request Nehemiah brought before the Lord was based on sure and certain promises God Himself had made. God had said that if His people were unfaithful, He would cast them into exile, and this is exactly what had happened to them (1:8). But this is not the whole story. Nehemiah brought before God the pledge God Himself made that when His people repented and returned to the Lord, He would restore them to their land. On the certainty of this promise Nehemiah placed his hope.

What stood behind this hope was the confidence that God is utterly true to His word. He is faithful. He is truthful. He is the original promise keeper! If God promised He would bring His people back to their land if they repented and turned again to Him, then God would do this, for God is faithful to His word.

Some views of God current in our churches lack this confidence that God is true to His word. Some hold that God cannot know the future in its entirety, and because of this, God may "predict" things about the future He simply cannot bring about. But clearly this was not Nehemiah's view, nor is it an accurate description of the God of the Bible. Rather, Nehemiah believed that if God said it, God would do it. Even if there were stubborn people inhabiting the land of Israel and oppressing Jerusalem, God was able to accomplish His will and fulfill His promise. On this solid ground of the faithfulness of God and His word Nehemiah staked his hope.

Nehemiah's prayer ends with an interesting and important twist. Notice, he did not merely call on God to "be attentive to the prayer of Your servant and to that of Your servants who delight to revere Your name" (v. 11); but he added, "Give Your servant success today, and have compassion on him in the presence of this man" (v. 11). Let's not miss this: Nehemiah shifted from simply thinking in terms of what God (alone) would do to fulfill this promise to how God might use Nehemiah as part of the answer to his own prayer. This was faith in action.

Nehemiah pictured for us not just confident faith in God, but also the desire and willingness for God to empower and use him in the fulfillment of the very request he brought before the Lord. What an example of dependence and determination, of trust and travail, of confidence and courage. May God grant us such vision—to "trust and obey, for there is no other way To be happy in Jesus, But to trust and obey."

For Your Consideration

1. Nehemiah based his confidence in God on God's sure and certain promises. Are you aware of promises of God that relate to specific challenges in your life? What are some? Have you searched the Scripture to see if God has promised certain things you can believe with confidence in the face of your trials?

2. Nehemiah trusted that God alone could bring victory, but he also was willing to put himself in the place of being used in bringing about that victory. What are some difficulties you've prayed about in which you need to ask God to grant you success? How can you envision yourself as part of the answer to your own prayers?

Taking Steps
of Faith

Bible Truth: *God strengthens those who act in faith in responding to spiritual challenges.*

Life Impact: *To help you take steps of faith in responding to spiritual challenges*

Courageous Commitment (Neh. 2:7-8)

How long is three months of waiting, wondering, and praying after hearing deeply distressing news that you have not been able to do anything about? How difficult is it to plead with God for an answer to some urgent and deeply felt prayer, and then to wait, day by day, week by week, even month by month, and receive no apparent response from the Lord? How well do we respond to delays (at least, that is what they seem to us to be) in God's answers to our prayers? Marvel, then, at Nehemiah's faith as told in the story that unfolds in chapters 2–3.

Imagine how the anguish of Nehemiah's heart must have felt. "During the month of Chislev," we are told, Nehemiah had been informed of the broken walls of Jerusalem and the discouragement of the Jews still

A CLOSER LOOK

Royal Prerogative

King Artaxerxes of Persia was not always in favor of the rebuilding of Jerusalem. Early in his reign, he received a letter from the Samaritan officials complaining about the Jewish efforts to rebuild the city. If allowed to finish, the letter said, the new Jerusalem residents would probably be nontax paying rebels against the king. Artaxerxes ordered the reconstruction halted (Ezra 4:11-23).

This same king later, in response to the sadness of his cupbearer Nehemiah, ordered the work resumed and even financed the project.

living there (1:1-3). Now as chapter 2 begins, three months have passed ("during the month of Nisan") before an opportunity was given Nehemiah to come into the presence of the king (v. 1).

As a cupbearer to the king, Nehemiah was called on to bring wine to King Artaxerxes. According to rules of expected behavior, the cupbearer was to be pleasant, humble, and not particularly noticeable as he brought in wine for the king. But times were not normal, and neither was Nehemiah. He came into the king's chambers different from ever before. He was obviously sad, and the king noticed.

For Nehemiah, this was both good news and bad news. The bad news was that since the cupbearer was not to appear sad in the king's presence, King Artaxerxes could have immediately commanded Nehemiah to be removed from his presence and executed. No wonder Nehemiah "was overwhelmed with fear" when he saw that the king noticed his sadness and even commented on it (v. 2). But the good news was apparent to Nehemiah right away. Because the king noticed Nehemiah's sadness and doubtless was convinced something must be seriously wrong, Artaxerxes allowed Nehemiah to express the reason for the distress of his heart and what he would request of the king. Incredible! What might have resulted in Nehemiah's immediate death instead began unfolding, before his eyes, as the beginning of the answer to his prayer. Just like that, after three months of pleading with God and waiting for God to act, Nehemiah was about to see God's hand move.

One of the most interesting details of this account is given in 2:4. "What is your request?" the king asked. The words that followed state simply, "So I prayed to the God of heaven and answered the king" (v. 4). Whoever said that prayers must be long and involved? Nehemiah could sense this was his big chance to secure the help he longed to have, and so immediately he prayed the only sort of prayer he could. We are not told the wording of this prayer, but I suspect it must been something along the lines of, "Oh God, please help! Please move the king's heart to hear and answer my request!"

Before moving from this little detail in the story, notice two related points: First, before Nehemiah said a word, he prayed! Clearly Nehemiah had a God-centered perspective on life. He evidently believed that whether the king would be receptive to his request or not was dependent ultimately not on what he said but on what God would do. He knew everything hinged on God's working. Even though we don't have Nehemiah's exact words, we do know that this very short prayer expressed his sincere hope and trust in God—believing that only God could bring about what he now sought.

Second, Nehemiah's prayer did not cancel out his responsibility to lay out his request before the king. Trustful prayer was followed by faithful action. Nehemiah prayed, then he spoke! Trusting God to do the work that He alone can do (Nehemiah prayed) and faithfully carrying out what we should do (Nehemiah answered the king)—both of these go together.

With boldness and confidence, Nehemiah told the king exactly what he wanted done: Provide official letters that permit me to travel to Jerusalem. Give me another letter that requests from others the building materials I will need. What forthrightness and confidence in God he showed that God would work in the king's heart to grant these requests. Clearly, Nehemiah was not trusting in his position before the king. These requests from the cupbearer were simply audacious and ridiculous. But because Nehemiah trusted God, he asked boldly.

And God answered. Some of the most important words of the whole book are recorded for us here: "The king granted my requests, for I was graciously strengthened by my God" (v. 8). Because God looked with favor on Nehemiah, He did work in the king's heart and brought about the response Nehemiah requested. Yes, Nehemiah was bold and trusting, but the king's response ultimately was the result of God's mercy and power.

The principle of Proverbs 21:1 is illustrated in this story: "A king's heart is a water channel in the LORD's hand: He directs it wherever He chooses." As Nehemiah boldly put aside his fear (Neh. 2:2) and turned instead in prayer to God (v. 3), God responded to his heart of trust and He did what only God can do: He moved the king's heart to look with favor on what Nehemiah requested of him.

What an amazing account. It is very much like a similar situation where Esther chose to appear before King Ahasuerus, knowing that such an uninvited appearance could bring her death ("If I perish, I perish," Esth. 4:16). Similarly here, Nehemiah knew his success in this matter would only happen because God worked in the king's heart. His trust in God was not in vain. God did so work, and the king did show Nehemiah favor by granting his requests. Such trust! And such divine power! What hope and confidence this should inspire in God's people for God to do what He alone can do.

For Your Consideration

1. When you face some difficulty, what is your first instinct? Do you pray? Or do you try to figure out

what to do? What can you learn from Nehemiah's reaction to the bad news he heard?

2. Give some specific examples from your life where you saw that trust in God and faithfulness in doing what you should do have worked together. What principles do you see in the story of Nehemiah that give guidance here?

3. As Nehemiah's story illustrates, God can move in the heart of even a king so the Lord's will is done through what the king says and does. How does this truth relate to problems you face? In particular, are there people in authority over you whom you can entrust to God that He will work in their hearts to accomplish His will?

Honest Appraisal and Bold Challenge (Neh. 2:11-18)

The story continues quickly. Nehemiah took the letters he had requested from King Artaxerxes and traveled west, across the Euphrates River. With him were officers and soldiers from the king's army, sent both to protect Nehemiah's company and to underscore the authority under which Nehemiah was sent (v. 9).

Illustrator Photo/Ken Touchton

Lion's (Stephen's) Gate, one of the entrances into the old city of Jerusalem.

Sanballat and Tobiah are now introduced to us. These two enemies of Israel were deeply dismayed to learn that Nehemiah had come, by the king's own orders, to seek the welfare of the Israelites who lived in Palestine (v. 10). Sanballat (the Horonite) was probably from the portion of central Israel, west of the Jordan River, called Samaria (compare 4:1-2) Tobiah (the Ammonite) was from just east of the Jordan River, opposite Samaria. These two men represented threats to Israel from both within and without its land, and they both were determined to foil any attempts to help Israel prosper. But because God was at work in Nehemiah's heart, no threats would deter this man from pursuing the calling God had given him.

Nehemiah arrived in Jerusalem and spent three days there before he began the work for which he had come (2:11). Why these three days? Why not plunge directly into the work at hand? No doubt Nehemiah knew the work he was considering would require the cooperation and commitment of most, if not all, the Israelites living in Jerusalem. So before facing them with his vision, he spent time in Jerusalem letting them get to know him and learning from them the condition of the life they endured.

In the secrecy of night Nehemiah and a few others took their evening tour of the walls of Jerusalem to see firsthand the extent of the disrepair. Wisely, Nehemiah did not yet reveal what he was thinking (v. 12). He waited until the right time to unfold both the burden and the plans of his heart. Knowing how much was at stake, he wanted others to join him in seeing for themselves afresh just how serious was the problem that he purposed to address.

Notice also a very interesting comment made in 2:12. "I got up at night and took a few men with me. I didn't tell anyone what my God had laid on my heart to do for Jerusalem." It is interesting and instructive that God's work in Nehemiah's heart (v. 12) actually preceded his tour of the fallen walls of Jerusalem (vv. 13-16), although he had already known secondhand of the disrepair of Jerusalem (1:3).

This illustrates the way God often works. God gives us a burden on the basis of some preliminary information, but before we know "all the facts," as it were. Then when we learn more, we see even more clearly and forcefully what perhaps even others had previously seen but had not acted on. Now with our eyes open to what God has shown us, God burns that vision ever more deeply into our minds and hearts.

Clearly, this was what happened to Nehemiah. Before his clandestine tour of the broken walls of Jerusalem, he already knew what God was prompting him to do. The tour of the walls that followed served to confirm and crystallize the importance of the vision God had already planted in his heart. Further, it also gave others the opportunity to see with Nehemiah just what was the basis of his burden.

Again we see how two things work together that we dare not separate. God worked in Nehemiah's heart to give him a vision of His will, *and* Nehemiah investigated the situation to learn better the nature of the challenge he faced. God's work in us to burden us with the vision He has for us, and our work to learn all we can about that vision—both of these go together. Great harm is done when we separate God's work in us from our responsibility to learn and labor in response to that divinely implanted vision.

The time came for Nehemiah to share his vision with others (2:17-18). Two crucial principles are evident from how Nehemiah proceeded. First, he shared his God-given vision with clarity and power (v. 17). No one listening to Nehemiah could possibly have walked away scratching his head, thinking, "I wonder what Nehemiah was talking about and just what it is he wants us to do." Rather, Nehemiah clearly and forcefully posed both the problem and a vision of the solution. If a leader expects others to follow, he must make clear and compelling his vision of what is wrong and what is needed to address that wrong.

Second, Nehemiah gave them strong reason to believe God would be with them in carrying out this vision (v. 18). Even if a leader makes his vision clear, if the people of God doubt whether God is behind their efforts, they will not be motivated to undertake the task with all of their hearts. Nehemiah knew the people needed to be assured that this was not merely his own idea, but God had confirmed over and again that this was His will. As Nehemiah put it, "I told them how the gracious hand of God had been on me, and what the king had said to me" (v. 18a). In other words, look at how clearly God has been both leading and empowering this work already. Doesn't this indicate clearly that God stands behind these efforts of rebuilding the walls? As a result, when the people understood the vision with clarity and forcefulness and when they were confident God willed that this work be done, they responded, "Let's start rebuilding" (v. 18b).

For Your Consideration

1. Are you in a position of leadership over others? What can you learn from how Nehemiah motivated and enlisted the help of these Israelites in accomplishing the vision God had given him?

Learning Activity

Proper Order

The steps Nehemiah took to remedy the problem of the broken wall can serve as a guide to us when we see a problem that needs to be fixed. Number the following steps from one to six in the order that they were taken by Nehemiah. Next to each step, write the verse numbers (from Neh. 2) that relate to that step.

_____ Develop a plan   Neh. 2: _____

_____ Obtain authorization   Neh. 2: _____

_____ Recognize a need   Neh. 2: _____

_____ Enlist others   Neh. 2: _____

_____ Personally commit   Neh. 2: _____

_____ Secure resources   Neh. 2: _____

2. How important is it to know that God is behind the labors that a leader is asking others to give? How would this story be different had Nehemiah received no such vision from the Lord, and yet he called these Israelites to join him in this work? How does this apply to your life and leadership?

3. Are you in a position of following the leadership of others? What lessons from Nehemiah can you apply to your role? If you are not clear either about the nature of the vision you are asked to share, or you are not convinced that God is behind it, what should you do?

A Good Beginning (Neh. 3:1-5)

By God's grace Nehemiah succeeded in persuading the Israelites of Jerusalem to see and own the vision the Lord gave him of rebuilding the wall. They had grasped the vision clearly, and they knew with confidence God was behind this plan. As one might expect, however, Nehemiah met with immediate opposition from the enemies of Israel. Sanballat, Tobiah, and another opponent, Geshem the Arab, challenged Nehemiah, charging him with rebelling against the king (2:19). Nehemiah did not fall for this baseless challenge. He had already given the letters from King Artaxerxes into the hands of the regional officials, and he knew that Sanballat and Tobiah knew this (3:9-10). Rather than wrangling over the legalities of his plan, he spoke directly to the rebel-

27

Learning Activity

"Let's Start Rebuilding"

After Nehemiah had shown them the need, the people responded: "Let's start rebuilding" (2:18). Then they each claimed a section of the wall and went to work. What needs in your church are you personally fulfilling? What needs could you help meet? In the following list, put a check mark by those you are already doing and a star by areas in which you would consider helping.

❏ Bible study leader

❏ Usher

❏ Choir member

❏ Office volunteer

❏ Clean up facilities

❏ Technology help

❏ Contacting prospects

❏ Repairs

❏ Instrumentalist

❏ Preschool care

❏ Greeter

❏ Yard work, landscaping

❏ Planning fellowships

❏ Painting

❏ Decorating

❏ _____

❏ _____

❏ _____

❏ _____

❏ _____

❏ _____

lion of their hearts and the certainty of God's plan. To these opponents of Israel he declared, "The God of heaven is the One who will grant us success. We, His servants, will start building, but you have no share, right, or historic claim in Jerusalem" (2:20).

What follows next is nothing short of remarkable. Nehemiah 3 records an extended list of those who undertook the work of repairing different sections of the walls and gates of Jerusalem. While one can get lost in the details (so many long and foreign names, and so many gates and parts of the wall), the main point is very clear: God moved the hearts of the vast majority of those who lived in and near Jerusalem to join together in this massive, difficult, and prolonged work of rebuilding the walls of Jerusalem. And how did God do this work in them? Through Nehemiah's faithful and courageous leadership.

Something very important should be evident from this story. Yes, it is true that God can move people's hearts directly to do His will, as He did with King Artaxerxes to look with favor on Nehemiah when he learned about the broken walls of Jerusalem (2:8). God simply could have directly moved the hearts of all of the Israelites to be burdened to rebuild the broken walls. Thus He would never have had to use Nehemiah to do this work. But this is not normally how God chooses to work. Rather, He worked first in Nehemiah's life, then in the heart of the king, and then through Nehemiah God moved the Israelites to join forces in rebuilding the walls.

Here's the point: God could have accomplished this without Nehemiah—He is God, after all! But God's usual way of accomplishing His will is through the ministry of His servants. Nehemiah was God's chosen instrument through whom He would move the people's hearts to do His will. How gracious God is to use us when He is fully able to work in any and every way He pleases on His own, apart from us. While God is responsible for enabling the work that is done, and while He receives all the glory for the good accomplished, God often chooses to fulfill His will and accomplish His work through His human instruments. God graciously shares with us the joy and responsibility of joining Him in His work.

Notice how broadly and widely God worked among the Israelites through Nehemiah's leadership. Nehemiah 3:1-5 sets the pattern for what is evident throughout the chapter. As you read through Nehemiah 3, you will notice over and again the places named from which various workers came, for example, "men of Jericho" (v. 2), "the Tekoites" (v. 5), "men of Gibeon and Mizpah" (v. 7), the "ruler over half the district of Jerusalem" (vv. 9,12), the "ruler over the district of Beth-haccherem" (v. 14), the "ruler over the district of Mizpah" (v. 15), the "ruler over half the district of Beth-zur" (v. 16), and so forth. So many people, from so many places, involving priests, nobles, numerous families, common people and regional leaders—all came together for the united purpose of joining in the labor of fulfilling the vision God brought to these people through Nehemiah. What a marvelous story of God's grace, involving His sovereign working through an obedient leader and involving such a vast array of people.

For Your Consideration

1. Do you sometimes think that if God is responsible for the work, then you're not? Or if you are responsible for the work, then God is not? What lessons can be learned from the story of Nehemiah to help see this issue as God would want us to?

2. Have you sometimes felt that as long as other people are involved in doing the work, you can sit back and relax? This may be correct some-times, but doesn't the story of Nehemiah make it clear that sometimes God expects all of God's people to get involved? Are there areas in the life of your church where this may be the case?

Overcoming Obstacles

Bible Truth: *Obstacles to God's work are inevitable. By trusting God and being determined to continue His work, God's people can find ways to overcome obstacles.*

Life Impact: *To help you overcome obstacles to God's work with faith and determination*

Fearful Threats (Neh. 4:6-23)

Nehemiah 4 is one of the highest points in all of the history of Israel, for it tells a riveting story of extraordinary hope and trust in God in the face of mounting, relentless, and wicked opposition to the people of God. Let's consider what transpires in this chapter and then draw out a number of lessons we can learn from this amazing account.

Sanballat and Tobiah come back into the picture. You'll recall that we were first introduced to them in Nehemiah 2:10 as the two key figures who stood determined to oppose any efforts to refortify the city of Jerusalem. Now in chapter 4 we learn they have heard that Nehemiah and numerous Israelites had joined together in an almost unbelievable begin-

A CLOSER LOOK

Sanballat and Tobiah

Who were Sanballat and Tobiah, the two men who sought to sabotage the rebuilding of Jerusalem's walls?

Sanballat, according to the Elephantine Papyri, was governor of Samaria. Although using a Babylonian name he probably was given during the exile, Sanballat was Jewish and his daughter was the wife of the high priest's grandson.

Tobiah was also Jewish and came from a family of wealthy landowners. He is thought to have been the governor of Ammon or some other high-ranking official of that area. After a trip to Babylon, Nehemiah was horrified to find the high priest had given Tobiah a room in the temple courtyard. Nehemiah had Tobiah and his belongings thrown out and the room cleansed for its proper use.

Together Sanballat and Tobiah did all they could to sabotage the rebuilding of the wall. They had personal selfish motives: the establishment of Jerusalem as the leading city in the area would threaten the political and economic advantages they enjoyed under the current situation.

ning of rebuilding Jerusalem's walls, and they are horrified. They mocked the faithful Israelites, making light of their efforts, and sarcastically dismissing their work as entirely futile and vain (4:1-3). Though Sanballat and Tobiah were in Samaria (quite a distance north of Jerusalem), news of their mocking words came to Nehemiah. Immediately Nehemiah did what he regularly did in the face of distressing news—he prayed.

Nehemiah clearly was a strong leader and exceedingly capable, yet more than this, he was a godly man. His trust was in the Lord, and he knew the only hope he and his Israelite brothers and sisters had was if the Lord would stand with them and against these forces of opposition. And, it was this realization that explains what might otherwise seem to us today a troubling prayer (vv. 4-5). In short, Nehemiah prayed for God to bring down Sanballat, Tobiah, and their coconspirators. What was so clear to

Nehemiah was that Sanballat and Tobiah had been scheming and plotting in ways directly opposed to the plans God had given the children of Israel to perform. Therefore, for God to support the faithful Israelites required that He stand against those who mocked and scorned His work. And for this, Nehemiah boldly prayed. Nehemiah's earlier confidence that "the God of heaven is the One who will grant us success" (2:20) is now expressed, on the flip side, by "Make their insults return on their own heads" (4:4).

Thankfully, Nehemiah's trust in God bore fruit. The people continued their laborious work of rebuilding the walls and gates of Jerusalem, and finally the wall was connected at every point around the city. Although it still needed to be made much higher, at least the whole of the wall was joined. What an accomplishment in a relatively short time, and it happened because "the people had the will to keep working" (v. 6). God's work in and through the courageous and compelling leadership of Nehemiah and God's work in the people who joined the work resulted in great initial success.

Most of us have experienced this next principle: Initial success is often followed by renewed and increasing opposition. So it was for Nehemiah and the faithful Israelites. Sanballat and Tobiah realized that their "war of words" through mocking and insults had not deterred the workers in Jerusalem, so they decided they must become more aggressive and direct in their opposition. They sent word throughout Judah (the region of Israel where Jerusalem was located) that they would come to fight against Jerusalem. In fact, they would come secretly and when least expected (vv. 11-12). This news had to have been greatly distressing. After all, although the wall had now been completely joined, it was very low in places and invaders could easily enter the city and begin killing the workers and their families. Discouragement set in, and it began to be spoken throughout Judah, "The strength of the

Learning Activity

Sources of Discouragement

As Nehemiah led his people to rebuild the wall, he constantly found himself having to deal with their feelings of discouragement. Which of the following factors have discouraged you from vigorously carrying out what you believed to be God's will?

❑ The enormity of the task
❑ Physical or emotional exhaustion
❑ Not seeing desired results
❑ Ridicule from those who don't understand
❑ Attempts by others to stop the work
❑ The distraction of personal problems
❑ Lack of support from others
❑ Sense of being disconnected from others working

Nehemiah never was one to recommend quitting. What steps do you think he would suggest you take to deal with your discouragement?

_____

_____

_____

_____

_____

laborer fails, since there is so much rubble. We will never be able to rebuild the wall" (v. 10).

Nehemiah's response in this distressing situation is both inspirational and instructive. Rather than despairing along with the people and resorting to a "self-esteem" message along the lines of, "You can do it if you just put your minds to it"—he directed the people's attention once again to God. Standing before all the nobles, officials, and the workers in Jerusalem, he proclaimed, "Don't be afraid of them. Remember the great and awe-inspiring Lord, and fight for your countrymen, your sons and daughters, your wives and homes" (v. 14). The combination of "remember ... the Lord" and "fight for your countrymen" is again both remarkable yet typical of how Nehemiah thought and acted. Remembering the greatness and power of God inspired and motivated the action he called forth from the people.

Evidently, the enemies of Israel were hoping that just the rumor of a possible military campaign against Jerusalem would discourage the workers and bring the rebuilding of Jerusalem to a standstill. But God worked through Nehemiah to strengthen the people's resolve. A very telling comment is made in Nehemiah 4:15: "When our enemies realized that we knew their scheme and that God had frustrated it ...." So their plan was for their threat to end the work in Jerusalem, but God "frustrated" this plan by using Nehemiah to inspire hope in the people.

As wonderful as it was that the Israelites had been moved by God to continue working, Nehemiah also knew their enemies had learned the work was continuing. What would he do now? Nehemiah surprises us even more by how strongly he believed that trust in God must be expressed by vigorous activity. Knowing that an attempted invasion of the city was a distinct possibility, Nehemiah ordered half of the workers on the wall to carry spears, shields, bows, and breastplates, while the other half continued the work. Many workers carried tools with one hand and a weapon in the other, and a trumpeter was stationed near Nehemiah, ready to sound the alarm for battle (vv. 16-18).

Learning Activity

Personal Reflection

Can you think of a time when you were striving to serve God faithfully but ran into obstacles? Briefly describe that situation by answering the following questions.

1. What were you trying to do?

2. What obstacle(s) stood in your way?

3. What steps did you take to overcome the obstacle(s)?

4. What was the final outcome?

Some might say this is evidence that instead of trusting in God Nehemiah was now trusting in his own strategies and in the military might of the Israelites. But clearly the narrative of this story leads us to conclude otherwise. With courage and great trust in God, Nehemiah proclaimed, "The work is enormous and spread out, and we are separated far from one another along the wall. Wherever you hear the trumpet sound, rally to us there. Our God will fight for us!" (vv. 19-20). Much like Joshua in the conquest of Palestine, Nehemiah believed that only because

God was with them and fought for them would they defeat with their meager force of arms whatever assault came against them. While Nehemiah made use of what military arsenal he had available, he had no pretenses that they could withstand a mighty military attack. While he stood ready as best he could, his hope was placed firmly and squarely in the Lord. And ultimately, it was the Lord and His strength to which Nehemiah pointed his people's attention. "Our God will fight for us!" would ring in their ears.

The strategy worked, and the people continued their work, prepared every moment for impending battle. The rebuilding of the wall continued (vv. 21-23). What could easily have brought their work to a halt failed because God was stronger than their opposition and the people were led to place their hope in God. Truly, this chapter is one of the most inspiring and remarkable accounts in the whole Bible, and there is much here for us to learn. Consider a few of the lessons God may have for us from Nehemiah 4.

First, obstacles to God's will and work are inevitable. If any of us suffers from the illusion that if we just follow the Lord's will we may anticipate ease and freedom from distress, we can learn here what is true throughout the Bible: God's faithful people can anticipate opposition. Obstacles will come in some form or another. Actually, one very common form of obstacle is the first kind that was thrust at Nehemiah and the faithful Israelites: mocking words of insult and discouragement. Since the greatest enemy of our faith is a liar from the beginning (John 8:44) and a deceiver (2 Cor. 11:3), we can anticipate that one of his chief weapons will be the unkind, hurtful, twisted, threatening words of those who stand against the work God has designed. Obstacles will come—whether through deceitful words or in other ways—and God's people are only prepared when they recognize and anticipate this hard reality.

Second, clarity of vision requires not only that we see what needs to be done but also that we see what stands against the accomplishment of the vision. Then we can resolve to oppose it. If the accomplishment of God's will normally meets with opposition, then it stands to reason we must resolve to defeat the opposition to fulfill the will of God. Nehemiah saw this with such clarity that his prayer early in chapter 4 focused specifically on God's defeat of the opposition. Just as one cannot truly and deeply love what is good without also hating what is evil (Rom. 12:9), so one cannot stand for the accomplishment of God's will without standing against all that rises up to oppose it. Nehemiah's courage and trust in God are shown precisely in both his standing for what is right and his standing against the threatening and serious opposition he faced.

Third, the immediate response of the godly to distress and opposition is prayer. Why prayer? Simply because nothing indicates more clearly and forcefully in what we are placing our hope and trust. If we respond to discouragement by immediately plotting how we will handle it—how we can overcome it—then we show that our hope is in ourselves (or in others whom we imagine we can manipulate to help us). But, if our hope truly is in God, we will do as Nehemiah regularly did when trials came. We will pray!

Fourth, even though Nehemiah prayed immediately after learning some distressing news, his prayers were always followed by concrete and wise actions. The lesson here is as profound as it is simple: Trusting God doesn't negate our responsible action. Rather, prayer and hope in God actually stimulate us to action in order to put "feet" to our faith. Over and again we see this principle expressed in Nehemiah's life. Here in chapter 4, Nehemiah's hope in God is followed by a plan of building the wall while being ready also for military attack. Trust in God and careful planning go hand in hand, as Nehemiah's call to the people in verse 14 illustrates: "Remember the great and awe-inspiring Lord...and fight." Neither one should cancel the other, and both together manifest the wisdom of how God often and regularly works in this world.

Fifth, success in the work of God comes through persistence and perseverance when facing hardship and opposition. Yes, sometimes God brings His people quick and immediate victories. But as one looks through the pages of Scripture, and clearly as one reads Nehemiah 4, we learn that God sometimes brings His people their sought-after success only through the long and hard pathway of persistent trust and persevering labor. Since God could bring immediate success every time, why might He choose more often to make our success prolonged and labored? Clearly from this account and many others we understand that God's people must continue trusting Him day by day, sometimes in greater measure as the opposition increases. Since God's goal is that we learn to trust Him, to hope in Him, to find our joy in Him, it often suits His purposes best to lead His people to success through the pathway of persevering faithfulness.

For Your Consideration

1. Consider your own expectations when deciding to follow God's will and engage in some aspect of His work. Does the thought of "opposition" enter your thinking? How would it help you in deciding what it means to follow God's will if you considered the reality that God's work is usually opposed?

2. How do you balance the "prayer" and "responsible action" aspects of the Christian life? When you face difficulties, do you respond to them as Nehemiah did? Do you tend to respond with one (prayer or action) without the other? Do you pray first? How do you assess your own responses to challenges that come to you?

3. Do you have a track record of persevering in the work God gives you to do? What do you tend to do when opposition comes? Do you give up, or do you trust God and resolve to continue "building the wall" until the work is done? How does Nehemiah's example help you in considering your own response to difficulties?

Unjust Practices (Neh. 5:1-13)

It is one thing to face opposition from without—as we've seen, we should expect that this might well happen. But when opposition comes from within the camp, this can be even more deeply demoralizing. So it was with Nehemiah and the Israelites within Jerusalem.

Greed is a powerful force, one facing all of us in various ways and to various extents. More accurately, greed is a powerful expression of our sinful natures. Those in positions of authority over others are the ones most prone to succumb to temptations of greed.

The story of Nehemiah 5:1-13 can be a bit confusing, but essentially this is what happened. The "widespread outcry" of verse 1 was directed against "their Jewish countrymen," who later we learn were the nobles and rulers within Jerusalem and its environs. Here, then, we do not have a complaint of faithful Jews against external enemies from without. Rather, this is a complaint of brother against brother, Jew against Jew, some of the workers in Jerusalem against others who, with them, were working to rebuild the wall. Those who were poorer and who had to borrow money to lease plots of land on which to grow their crops were deeply distressed that they had to pay excessive usury (that is, interest) payments to the nobles and rulers who loaned them this money.

The forms of the usury payments are indicated in Nehemiah 5:3-5. Some had actually mortgaged their fields in order to acquire the money needed to make their usury payments. Others had sold the very crops their families needed to eat because they didn't have the money exacted by the nobles. Still others resorted to selling themselves or some of the members of their families as slaves to acquire the money needed to make their usury payments. And evidently, even while the work had been conducted on the rebuilding of the walls of Jerusalem, the nobles and rulers had continued to demand that their usury payments be made.

When Nehemiah learned of this widespread complaint and the excessiveness of the charges, he became "extremely angry" (v. 6). He called the nobles and rulers together and confronted them directly. "Each of you is charging his countrymen interest" (v. 7), he stated in dismay to these leaders. Further, he pointed out the sad and deeply distressing irony that at the very same time when they were working to rebuild Jerusalem so the people of Israel might escape their slavery to other nations, here in Israel itself, the poor among the Jews were selling themselves as slaves to other Jews, in the very land of freedom (v. 8)!

The unfairness and unkindness of the actions of the nobles and rulers were painfully clear. When Nehemiah called them to "walk in the fear of our God and not invite the reproach of our foreign enemies" (v. 9), no doubt they could see immediately that their charging of usury was directly contrary to the very goals and purposes to which they were now committed in the rebuilding of Jerusalem. Surely, this practice had to stop, and Nehemiah called them to do so immediately.

Not only did Nehemiah call them to stop collecting usury, but furthermore, he called them to return past payments of usury, whether in the form of crops or mortgaged land or groves or houses or grain or wine and oil. Though the rich had become richer through this practice, Nehemiah called them not only to stop the practice but to restore enormous amounts of wealth to the people from whom it had been taken (vv. 10-11).

What response might we expect in a comparable situation today? Can't we just imagine the endless explanations and rationalizations given by those who had profited from the practice? Wouldn't we expect strong resistance, since the rich were being asked not only to give up the practice that had brought them increasing wealth but to give back a large portion of that wealth itself?

Amazingly, God's grace was shown abundantly in Nehemiah's day. Rather than protesting Nehemiah's call to them, rather than justifying what they had been doing, they responded in a way only possible when God is at work: "We will return these things and require nothing more from them," they said. "We will do as you say" (v. 12). Grace is seldom more amazing than when it touches our pocketbooks. What an amazing display of grace is manifest here!

But Nehemiah showed he knew that by nature his people were fickle. He knew that even with the best of intentions, they might promise something they would later take back. So, rather than just leaving things there, he went one step further. He summoned the priests to come so all the nobles and rulers might take an oath before the Lord promising that if they did not do as they said, God may take from them their own houses and property. Nehemiah himself symbolized this by shaking the folds of his robe, indicating the kind of shaking God would do to any who went back on this pledge. Once again, even after calling them to promise and presenting them with this threat, the rulers and nobles and whole assembly still embraced the oath and went forward to carry out what they promised (v. 13).

How remarkably this contrasts with so many of our disputes within the church. And how much we need God's work in our midst so when correction or rebuke comes, God will prepare the hearts of the wrong-doers to be desirous of change. May we be faithful and obedient as Nehemiah was so God will display such power and grace in our midst today.

For Your Consideration

1. Are you aware of unfair or unkind practices taking place between believers in the church today? What steps should be taken to stop these practices and bring restitution?

2. Isn't there a clear connection between God's work of grace in our lives and how we think of our money? If God worked in us as He did in those of Nehemiah's day, what changes might this require of us in our use of the money God gives us?

Finishing God's Work

Bible Truth: *God provides His people all they need to accomplish the work He gives them to do.*

Life Impact: *To help you discover and finish the work God has for you*

Strength to Avoid Distractions (Neh. 6:1-14)

Even the wisest and most godly of men and women can be led away from the work God has called them to do by listening to distracting voices. Voices that pull us away from what we should be doing can call from many quarters. Sometimes these voices sound legitimate, yet they call us in a direction opposite to what God has called us to do. We need divine discernment and spiritual insight if we are to stay on course and finish God's work.

In Nehemiah's case, not only were the voices calls to distract and to postpone the completion of his God-ordained work, but he soon found out that these were malicious voices intended to bring harm to him and to his character. Nehemiah 6 records a series of voices of distraction

A CLOSER LOOK

The Importance of Character in Leadership

When Nehemiah looked for a leader to put in charge of the newly walled city of Jerusalem, he decided on his brother (whom he surely knew well) and a man named Hananiah, "because he was a faithful man who feared God more than most" (Neh. 7:2). The New International Version refers to Hananiah as "a man of integrity."

Spiritual leadership is dependent more on character than on skill, experience, and personality. Techniques of leadership can be learned and tools of leadership can be acquired, but the person we trust to lead us must, first of all, be a godly person who knows God intimately.

When the apostles needed help with a church situation, they told the congregation to choose leaders "of good reputation, full of the Spirit and wisdom" (Acts 6:3). When Paul told Timothy what kind of person would make a good overseer for a church, he emphasized things such as "above approach," "respectable," and "good reputation among outsiders" (1 Tim. 3:2-7).

With that kind of raw material with which to work, God can create a strong and effective leader.

meant to hinder the completion of the rebuilding of Jerusalem's walls. Some of these calls to Nehemiah have a ring of legitimacy, so we learn here how subtle and deceitful these voices that call us away from the will of God can be.

Learning Activity

Discerning Motives

To the outside observer, the messages to Nehemiah recorded in chapter 6 might look like attempts to help him. Nehemiah knew better; he discerned the wicked motives behind the offers of help. Look through Nehemiah 6 and find out what agendas were really behind the messages.

Nehemiah 6:2 They were planning to

Nehemiah 6:3 They wanted the work to

Nehemiah 6:8 They were inventing and spreading

Nehemiah 6:9 They were trying to

Nehemiah 6:9 They hoped to

Nehemiah 6:13 They wanted Nehemiah to

First, we encounter Sanballat, Tobiah, and Geshem again (6:1; compare 2:19), the long-standing enemies of Nehemiah and of the faithful workers in Jerusalem. These wicked men had heard that all the breaches of the walls had been restored and that the work of rebuilding Jerusalem's walls was close to completion. Previous attempts to hinder this work had failed, so now these men plotted to send a message to Nehemiah that he leave Jerusalem and come and meet with them.

Nehemiah rightly discerned the malice in their invitation and refused to leave. Repeated invitations were answered with the same reply. Honestly, one must wonder about the intelligence of these three men. Just why they would think Nehemiah would be lured to meet them away from Jerusalem, when all they had done was oppose and threaten the rebuilding work he was leading, is difficult to figure. Perhaps this shows just how desperate people can become when frustrated by failure, as no doubt these enemies were. In any case, this attempt to distract Nehemiah from completing his work was fairly easily set aside. He discerned from the outset their intent was only harm (6:2).

Second, after four failed attempts to get Nehemiah to leave Jerusalem to meet them elsewhere, Sanballat sent a letter to Nehemiah accusing him of plotting rebellion against the king of Babylon and of planning to proclaim himself king over Judah. Clearly, this would have been a serious charge were it true. To plot rebellion against Babylon and to proclaim himself king in Judah would have been the most flagrant insubordination Nehemiah could commit against the very king (King Artaxerxes) who first sent him back to Jerusalem and granted him letters and military escort to assist his mission.

Sanballat's letter must have irritated Nehemiah greatly, since he would have understood the gravity of the charges and he would have wanted to vindicate himself by proving them false. But to turn from his work and travel to declare that these charges were false would have postponed the work's completion, and it also would have drawn him away from the city and made him more vulnerable. So rather than engage Sanballat on the basis of these charges, he did the much simpler and easier thing: Nehemiah called his bluff! He replied to Sanballat, "There is nothing to these rumors you are spreading; you are inventing them in your own mind" (v. 8). And through this, again, Nehemiah real-

ized that these enemies were only trying to distract him from the work God had given him and to hinder its completion. So having faced yet this second attempted barrier, he turned again to God in prayer and requests, "But now, my God, strengthen me" (v. 9).

Third and most deceptive, Shemaiah, a prophet of the Lord, spoke to Nehemiah and warned him to flee into the temple and close the doors, for his enemies were coming to kill him in the night. As the story unfolds, we learn that this prophet had been hired by Sanballat and Tobiah to trick Nehemiah into doing something that would bring God's judgment on him and ridicule from the Israelites. As Nehemiah put it, Shemaiah "was hired, so that I would be intimidated, do as he suggested, sin, and get a bad reputation, in order that they could discredit me" (v. 13). Probably in

The Wailing Wall is the only remaining wall of the ancient temple area in Jerusalem.

Illustrator Photo/Ken Touchton

the background of this statement is the commandment given in Numbers 18:7 that God would put to death any outsider or foreigner who entered the temple. Nehemiah knew that it was no light matter to enter the temple, and so to go there to flee would be to bring discredit to his own character before the people.

Nehemiah saw through this ruse, and he refused to go. He learned his enemies hired Shemaiah to trick him. So he prayed once more to God: "My God, remember Tobiah and Sanballat for what they have done, and also Noadiah the prophetess and the other prophets who wanted to intimidate me" (v. 14). The only way Nehemiah could hope to avoid stumbling by such tricks was if the Lord stood with him and stood against his enemies.

His prayer was answered as the wall was completed—all within a full 52 days of hard and persistent labor (v. 15). Nehemiah was careful to give credit ultimately to God. It must have been with great joy that he recorded, "When all our enemies heard this, all the surrounding nations were intimidated and lost their confidence, for they realized that this task had been accomplished by our God" (v. 16). Having avoided the distractions, the traps, and the deceitful schemes, Nehemiah rejoiced at the faithfulness of God to enable the wall's completion.

For Your Consideration

1. As you look back on your life, what distractions have come your way, tempting you to turn aside from what God was calling you to do? Have these distractions succeeded? How might you even now resolve to complete the work God has directed for you?

2. How do you think Nehemiah was so able to see through the schemes of his enemies and stay on track? What factors from the previous chapters of the book might help us see how he was able so clearly to stay focused on what God had called him to do? How might this relate to your life and calling?

Wisdom About Important Details (Neh. 6:15—7:3)

For a man who trusted God as fully and thoroughly as Nehemiah did, we also observe him often using his head and making many important decisions. As we have seen so often, trust in God and responsible action do not conflict; and certainly in the life and story of Nehemiah these two go hand in hand.

In the brief section opening chapter 7, Nehemiah had focused on how the people of Jerusalem should live peacefully and securely in the city since the wall had been completed. With the wall fully rebuilt and the doors and gates all in place, immediately he set his mind on what would be needed to secure the city and how God might be honored in this.

As one might expect, Nehemiah was primarily concerned with appointing gatekeepers and guards for the security and protection of the city. But along with these he also appointed singers and Levites to be stationed at the wall (v. 1). Clearly, this was an unusual move. Singers and Levites were to be appointed to serve at the temple, but now in light of the present distress and need for God's special protection, Nehemiah appointed singers and Levites to be placed along the wall. No doubt Nehemiah wanted these men to serve as symbols of prayer and joy surrounding the city. The Levites would intercede for the city and the singers would lead in songs of praise, assuring the people that the Lord was with them. Although this was an unusual move, it fits what we have come to see about Nehemiah's godly character and hope and trust in the Lord.

Next, Nehemiah was concerned for the appointment of godly, faithful men to place in command of the city as a whole. The main criterion that concerned Nehemiah, and the reason he selected Hananiah, in particular, was that he was "a faithful man who feared God more than most" (v. 2). A leader like Nehemiah must have confidence in the people he chooses, and what gave Nehemiah the greatest assurance about the men leading the city was their character.

Finally, Nehemiah provided some very specific instructions regarding the opening and shutting of the gates of the city. He ordered, "Do not open the gates of Jerusalem until the sun is hot, and let the doors be shut and securely fastened while the guards are on duty. Station the citizens of Jerusalem as guards, some at their posts and some at their homes" (v. 3). The most curious feature in these instructions was waiting until the sun was hot to open the gates. Likely, his concern was that the gates not be opened prematurely early, before the new guards had come to their posts and before there was full light of day to ensure that no strangers were able to slip inside the walls. This precaution shows us just how thoughtful Nehemiah was to details he knew could make a difference in the safety and security of the city.

For Your Consideration

1. Notice the balance in the details between matters of personal character and matters of sheer pragmatic importance. Do you see in some leaders at times a tendency to care about one of these and not the other? How important is it to care about both the character of those put in leadership and the very specific practical matters?

2. Have you heard the phrase "The details matter"? Or what about "Don't bother me with details"? Which expression is closer to the truth and why?

Acknowledgment of Others' Contributions (Neh. 7:4-5a,66-73a)

Having secured the wall and put in charge men to oversee the city, Nehemiah might now relax, one might think. Finally! The past several months had been exceedingly stressful, with more challenges than he probably had faced ever before in his life. Surely, the time had come to take a break.

But while the main objective—rebuilding the wall and making it secure for the inhabitants of Jerusalem—was accomplished, we immediately find out that all was not well and more work must be done. Right after the note of finality struck with the appointing of the guards and those who would lead the city (vv. 1-3) follows this interesting observation: "The city was large and spacious, but there were few people in it, and no houses had been built yet" (v. 4). This is more than a simple statement of fact thrown into the passage. No, this is a clue from the book's author that while the city was secure and its leaders appointed, much work still needed to be done in the city itself for it to become a place where the people of God could prosper. The goal of reclaiming the wall of the city surely was so the city would again become the glorious place God intended it to be, where temple worship would again take place and where His presence would be exhibited among His people. No, the work was not over, and God continued to use Nehemiah to accomplish what He intended to bring to completion.

It is no surprise, then, that the very next verse reads as it does: "Then my God put it into my mind to assemble the nobles, the officials, and the people to be registered by genealogy" (v. 5a). Once again, God is credited with working in and through Nehemiah to advance His plans. As is true throughout the book, God Himself is the ultimate power at work, and He accomplished His work through His servants, particularly through the leadership He inspired in Nehemiah. The words summarizing the previous accomplishment of the completion of the wall are still fresh in our minds, "for they realized that this task had been accomplished by our God" (6:16), and now we read in like manner, "my God put it into my mind to assemble " (7:5a). No one need wonder who is ultimately responsible for the triumphs and successes recorded in this book.

Why, we might ask, did God put it in Nehemiah's mind to assemble the people in order to enroll them? It seems that two main goals were accomplished with this action. First, God's hand had been mightily at work in showing His mercy and blessing to the people of Israel by bringing them back to the land. God had made clear to Israel that when they obeyed Him, part of the blessing they would enjoy would be living in the land He had given them. Consider, for example, the promised blessings Moses made clear to the people: "The LORD will grant you a blessing on your storehouses and on everything you do; He will bless you in the land the LORD your God is giving you" (Deut. 28:8), and "The LORD will make you prosper abundantly with children, the offspring of your livestock, and your soil's produce in the land the LORD swore to your fathers to give you" (v. 11). Consider Moses' words just a few verses later that if they disobey the Lord, "The LORD will bring you and your king that you have appointed to a nation neither you nor your fathers have known, and there you will worship other gods, of wood and stone. You will become an object of horror, a scorn, and ridicule among all the peoples where the LORD will drive you" (28:36-37). So God's blessing on the people of Israel was clearly shown by God's prospering them in their own land, and God's judgment on Israel was manifest by God's driving them out of their land and into other foreign nations.

But this is not all that God promised Israel, as it pertains to their dwelling in their own land. He also made a promise that He would not ultimately leave His people in the land of foreigners and of foreign gods. Rather, the day would come when He would bring them back to their own land and work in them so they would become worshipers of God from their hearts. Consider, for example, God's wondrous promise to Israel, that He would again bless them and restore them: "For I will take you from the nations and gather you from all the counties and bring you into your own land. I will also sprinkle clean water on you, and you will be clean. I will cleanse you from all your impurities and all your idols" (Ezek. 36:24-25). God's renewed blessing necessarily involved, then, taking the Israelites out of the nations where He sent them and bringing them back into their own land, the land of God's promised presence and blessing.

God put it into Nehemiah's mind, therefore, to conduct a roll call of all the people of Israel who had returned from Babylon. The result was a wonderful confirmation that God was again showing blessing to His people. Look over Nehemiah 7:6-72 and marvel at all those who had returned! Surely, this tally of the people was greatly encouraging—God was keeping His promise—His blessing was returning to His people— and they might anticipate future days of peace and prosperity as God watched over His people in their own land.

Second, the roll call of the Israelites also demonstrated how wide had been the involvement of the people in the work of the Lord! The wall was rebuilt, Jerusalem was once again fortified and secure, and the participants in this great work included scores and scores of families throughout the land of Judah. These had been blessed to return from Babylon, and then God blessed them further by putting it in their hearts to devote themselves to this demanding and dangerous labor. Only because so many participated was the task completed. Surely God put it in Nehemiah's mind to number the people, in part, to demonstrate how widely the Lord had moved in inspiring His work to be done. Nehemiah and all the people could marvel at the extent of His grace in using so many to accomplish such a great work.

For Your Consideration

1. God put it into Nehemiah's mind to do something that would demonstrate the extent of God's work among His people. Can you think of ways you could demonstrate before others how God is at work? How might God be honored in your family, your church, by showing ways He is at work?

2. We've all heard the phrase "Many hands make light work," and yet we also know that the work of God is all too often done by few hands. What will it take in your church for people to catch a vision of the glory and happiness that could result if more people participated in the work of God? What hinders more people from getting involved? What can be done to address this problem?

Learning Activity

Building for a Reason

Once the wall was rebuilt and the doors installed, Nehemiah was struck by the emptiness of the city. Now the city needed to be filled with people, and taking a genealogical survey was the first step toward that end.

What could your church do to draw more people into your fellowship?

• Take a survey of the community and follow up on prospects
• Increase visibility
• Meet needs of those outside the church
• Involve more members in outreach

• _____

• _____

• _____

• _____

• _____

• _____

• _____

• _____

• _____

• _____

Renewing Your Worship

Bible Truth: *God's people strengthen their worship as they hear and obey God's Word, and they find new joy in knowing God.*

Life Impact: *To help you regularly seek renewal of your worship of God*

Attentiveness to God's Word
(Neh. 7:73b-8:8)

Can you imagine the same sort of thing happening today as is recorded in Nehemiah 8? My, how remarkable this is! In Nehemiah 8:1 we read that all the people gathered and asked Ezra the scribe to bring out the book of the law of Moses so he could read it to them and explain what it said. The people as a whole, that is, requested to hear God's laws read and explained to them, and they stood for hours and days with hearts eager to learn what God required of them! There probably is no greater evidence of the work of God's grace within a community of faith than when the people long to hear and learn the Word of God. This becomes the basis (as

A CLOSER LOOK

Revivals and Spiritual Awakenings

What does it take to have a revival among God's people or a spiritual awakening in a community?

Dr. J. Edwin Orr studied and wrote about revivals and awakenings in the Bible and throughout history. He reported that the Welsh Revival, which started in 1904, was sparked by the simple message of a 26-year-old coal miner studying for the ministry. After praying, "O God, bend me," Evan Roberts told the head of his college that he felt compelled to leave school and speak to the young people in his home church. He was granted permission. But when he told his home pastor he had "come to preach," the pastor was skeptical.

The pastor allowed Roberts to address any willing to remain after a Monday evening prayer meeting. Seventeen stayed, heard his message, and responded. The pastor then gave Roberts permission to speak the next evening, and the next. He preached all week, then a second week. As the crowds grew, Roberts continued to preach for five months, during which time 100,000 trusted Christ.

Orr reported that the revival had such an impact on the community that crime became nonexistent, drunkenness was cut in half, taverns went bankrupt, and the illegitimate birth rate dropped 44 percent. The revival swept Britain, Scandinavia, Germany, North America, Australia, Africa, Brazil, Mexico, and Chile.

What was the powerful message of that young preacher God used to bring revival? Here is a summary of what he preached:

"I have a message for you from God. You must confess any known sin to God and put any wrong done to others right. Second, you must put away any doubtful habit. Third, you must obey the Spirit promptly. Finally, you must confess your faith in Christ publicly."

we'll see later) for heartfelt contrition and earnest recommitment to follow God's will and ways. Marvel, then, at the work of grace accomplished among the Israelites in Jerusalem in Nehemiah's day.

Our section begins with this brief comment, "When the seventh month came and the Israelites had settled in their towns" (7:73b). Two observations regarding the significance of the "seventh month" are needed. First, the mention of the seventh month (month of Tishri in the Jewish calendar) indicates that the events that follow in chapter 8 took place just a few days after the completion of Jerusalem's wall. We were told earlier that the wall had been completed "on the twenty-fifth day of the month Elul" (6:15), and Elul was the sixth month of the year. At the beginning of the seventh month (8:2), then, the people showed an eagerness to learn the law of the Lord and to follow what His word taught. No doubt they were still overwhelmed at God's obvious gracious and powerful work among them to enable the completion of the wall in a mere 52 days, and this amidst significant threat and opposition. They were deeply thankful to God and they understood the genuine sense of indebtedness they owed Him. So they were eager to learn from Him and to follow His voice.

Second, Nehemiah 8 ends with the people conducting "an assembly, according to the ordinance" (v. 18). This is a reference to the assembly God required to be conducted on the eighth day of the seventh month, as described and commanded in Numbers 29 (see esp. Num. 29:35-38). The people's eagerness to listen to the law of the Lord and to follow His ways bore fruit. They learned exactly what they were to be doing on the very month of the year that the law commanded them to conduct special ceremonies. And for the first time since the days of Joshua (see Neh. 8:17), God's people were obeying His word and keeping His commandments. How gracious of God to move the people to long to learn His word at the very time they needed to be carrying out what it commanded. They learned what the law required, and immediately they performed what they were told to do, "and there was tremendous joy" (v. 17).

Learning Activity

Draw a Picture

In the space below, draw a simple picture depicting the scene described in Nehemiah 8:1-6. You don't need to be an artist; use simple figures. Then answer the following questions:

1. If you had been there that day, which one of the figures would you want to represent you? Mark it with a star.

2. What thoughts and feelings do you think you would have had during that experience? List them here:

What an amazing account this is. Notice a few features of the verses we are here studying. First, Nehemiah 8:3 indicates that those who gathered to hear God's word read were "the men, the women, and those who could understand" and that "all the people listened attentively." How amazing this is! And what a sight this must have been. Thousands of men, women, and children gathered (standing much of the time), attentively listening to the law of the Lord read and explained to them. Imagine if your church called special day-long meetings to gather to hear the Word of God read and taught, and if the vast majority of the older adults, younger adults, teens, and older children of your church all came and stood for hours and days listening attentively to what God had to say to them. As we all know well, if we want a crowd to gather these days, nearly always this requires some form of entertainment—and this is true even in our churches. But marvel here at such clear evidence of God's gracious work among His people. They had an earnest longing and hunger to hear God's word spoken and taught. May God bring such revival to our churches.

Second, the listing of names in verses 4 and 7 could be puzzling. Why include this detail about all of these men who stood with Ezra and participated on this day? Here is the point: Not only were the people eager to hear the law of God read and explained, but all of the leaders also participated and assisted in the detailed explanation of the law.

Perhaps one might think of the analogy this way: special Bible study meetings have been called at your church and not only did the people come out in great numbers, but the elders and deacons all showed up too! As any pastor will tell you, one of the most discouraging aspects of ministry can occur when, despite excitement among the people for what God is doing, the elders and deacons and other lay leadership of the church are uninvolved and apathetic. But this was not the case in Israel during these days of revival. These lists of names, which may seem unimportant and irrelevant, actually indicate how pervasive God's grace and work had spread. All of the people, along with all of Nehemiah's and Ezra's leaders, were eager to participate in the great work God was doing.

Third, marvel at what captivated the attention of the Israelites in Jerusalem. Ezra and others read from and explained the law of Moses to the people. Do you realize that this means reading and explaining books like Exodus, Leviticus, and Numbers? The first five books of our Bible contain "the law of Moses" (8:1) and this was what the people listened to with attentiveness and eagerness over these days. How much richness is there in God's Word that we simply do not know? How many precious jewels of truth and blessing are left buried in the pages of those seemingly dusty Old Testament books? What will it take for us today to become eager to learn from the whole of the Bible what God has revealed about Himself and His ways? Will the day ever come when we beg our pastors to preach longer and to work hard at digging out the riches of God's truth from all of the Bible?

This happened in Nehemiah's day, and what grace it was. The people's response was not boredom or tedium, but rather, "with their hands uplifted all the people said, 'Amen, Amen!' Then they bowed down and worshiped the LORD with their faces to the ground" (v. 6). May God grant us, in our churches, longings of heart for His Word, may we know the joy and strength of His truth, and may we be moved to worship Him as never before.

For Your Consideration

1. What is the level of your appetite for the Word of God? How would you characterize it: hungry from time to time? starving? seldom interesting in eating? To what would you attribute the current state of your spiritual appetite?

2. What do you think might happen in your life, and in your church, if people began reading the Word of God much more than they now do? What would happen if much more time was devoted to careful teaching of God's Word? Do you think God would want this to happen?

3. Do you see a connection between hunger for the Word of God and worship (vv. 5-6)? Why might more reading and teaching of the Word of God lead to richer and spontaneous worship?

Joy of the Lord
(Neh. 8:9-12)

Without a doubt, an amazing story only becomes more amazing! Hearing the law of the Lord read and explained to them could not have failed to expose many sins and transgressions of which the people of Jerusalem became painfully aware. It must have grieved them deeply to hear over and again what God commanded of them only to realize how much both they and their ancestors had turned away from God and His Word. As will become apparent in the next chapter (chap. 9), all the people were deeply moved to confess sin and take steps of recovery. The law of God had rightly moved them to mourning and weeping over their past failures as God's people.

But Nehemiah, Ezra, and the Levites believed that the people's mourning was premature. Clearly, in light of what happens in the next chapter, their mourning and deep contrition were right and necessary, but perhaps premature. Amazingly, the first response these godly leaders encouraged (required!) of the people was that they eat the best of foods, drink sweet and refreshing drink, share freely with those who lacked, and in all of this rejoice! As Nehemiah told them, "Go and eat what is rich, drink what is sweet, and send portions to those who have nothing prepared, since today is holy to our Lord. Do not grieve, because your strength comes from rejoicing in the LORD" (8:10).

We can learn a couple of related lessons from this interesting account. First, deep sorrow over sin and confession of our failures need to be done in a context of confidence in God's goodness and lavish kindness. That is, we must know how good God is, how much He wants our best, how generous and lavish He is to us, how deep is His longing that we are filled with joy—we must know all of this as the basis of our confession of sin before Him. Why? Simply because, if we confess sin unconvinced of God's goodness, we will not be inclined to genuinely turn from that sin to God in obedience, trust, and hope. Our bedrock confidence in God's goodness is essential for us to turn *from* our sin and *to* Him. To put this differently, what will most effectively and fully turn our hearts to God is not (in itself) seeing what is wrong with our sinful ways. As bad as sin is, seeing our sin will not work to turn our hearts toward God. Rather, what will turn us with eagerness and joy toward the Lord, with hearts longing to trust and obey Him, is the deep confidence that He is absolutely good and that His ways are those that lead us into the pathway of true and lasting joy. Nehemiah spoke such a rich and profound truth when he said, "your strength comes from rejoicing in the LORD" (v. 10).

Second, and stemming from the first point, holiness and happiness do not conflict with one another; rather, they go together! Isn't it amazing, and doesn't it sound odd to our ears, to hear Nehemiah say, "eat what is rich, drink what is sweet, and send portions to those who have nothing prepared, *since today is holy to our Lord*" (v. 10). Holiness is not stodginess! God's holiness does not make God a kill-joy! Rather, God wants His people to know that the holy life is the happy life. Nehemiah reinforced this truth in commanding the people to throw a party because this day was *holy* to the Lord!

How much we have misrepresented the concept of holiness in our lives and churches. For most of us, we connect "holy" with what is drab, dull, unpleasant, and lifeless. All one needs do is walk through a meadow of wild flowers or hike up through towering fir trees or sit in amazement watching the tide come crashing against rugged rocks to realize that the God of such beauty, such creativity, such richness and color and variety, is anything but dull. And this God is infinitely holy. Holiness and richness of life at its best are one and the same life.

Oh, how we need to know God as He is. How much we need to understand the richness and beauty of His character and ways. Lest confession of sin cloud the goodness and glory of the God who calls us to turn from sin back to Himself, may we recall to mind often one of the most precious truths God has given His people: "Give thanks to the Lord, for He is good. *His love is eternal* (Ps. 136:1).

For Your Consideration

1. Have you grown in your life with the Lord to have great confidence in God's full goodness? What relationship is there between confidence in God's goodness and living before Him with trust and obedience?

2. Have you ever wanted to turn from some sin but ended up going back to it? Why do you think this happens? Do you think we would be more successful in turning from sin if, in the process, we turned to something better? How can we grow to see God as "better"?

Celebration by Obedience
(Neh. 8:13-18)

My, how these people in Jerusalem longed for the word of God! Even after standing for days and listening to the law of the Lord read and explained and after their joyous celebration with rich food and sweet drink, now we read in Nehemiah 8:13 that the fathers of families and leaders of the land gathered to learn yet more from the law. Ezra's job of reading and explaining went on, and the leaders especially were singled out as responsible to learn and apply what the law said. One lesson in this account is as important as it is obvious: while all of God's people need to learn the Word of God, there is a special responsibility and obligation given to leaders (including fathers who are leaders of their families) to learn God's Word so as to lead their people in God's ways. So, it is significant that the focus now shifted from the masses of the people to the family leaders, and other leaders, as they submitted to more instruction and deeper understanding of what God had revealed.

What God especially directed them to learn about was of critical importance to the very month and time that this happened. Evidently, they were reading and learning from Leviticus 23 and Numbers 29 about various feasts God required. In the midst of this study, they learned that the current month they were in, the seventh month, was to be a time when the Feast of Booths was to be celebrated. In obedience to God, they read carefully what was required and then they proclaimed throughout Judah that the people should gather branches to make booths, as the law required (Neh. 8:14-15). The people responded en mass! Again, what wonder there is throughout this chapter as God's grace to move these people to obedience is so richly evident. The result was nothing short of amazing. As Nehemiah recorded it, "The whole community that had returned from exile made booths and lived in them. They had not celebrated like this from the days of Joshua son of Nun until that day. And there was tremendous joy" (v. 17).

As we learn in Leviticus 23, the Feast of Booths was to be celebrated seven days, ending with an eighth day of holy convocation (Lev. 23:34-36). During these days, there was to be no regular work (v. 36) but the people were to celebrate and rejoice (vv. 39-40). The Feast of Booths was to conclude with a holy convocation or solemn assembly in which offerings were presented to the Lord with fire (v. 36), and the people were to remember that God had delivered them from their slavery in Egypt and had brought them out to live in the land of His choosing, a land of plenty and a place of God's blessing.

The purpose of living in these make-shift tents (booths) for the seven days is made clear at the end of Leviticus 23: "so that your generations may know that I made the Israelites live in booths when I brought them out of the land of Egypt; I am the LORD you God" (v. 43). The annual Feast of Booths, then, was to remind the people of Israel of their identity as those redeemed by God from slavery in Egypt and as the people whom God provided for in bringing them into the land of His promised blessing.

How wonderful that now, after all these years, the people of Israel were finally celebrating this glorious, joy-filled, worship-inspiring feast. We should recall—when we read that Israel "had not celebrated like this from the days of Joshua son of Nun until that day" (Neh. 8:17)—that this means for nearly 1,000 years of Jewish history, this command of God had gone neglected, the joy associated with this feast unfulfilled. The conquest of the land of Palestine under Joshua's leadership took place about 1400 B.C. This account in Nehemiah 8 occurred about 445 B.C. After such a long negligence, how gracious of God to lead them to learn about and celebrate this feast of such great joy.

And of course the symbolism could not have been any richer. The Feast of Booths was a reminder of how God cared for His people as they anticipated entering the promised land. But for Nehemiah and his people, they could look back at how God preserved them during their exile in Babylon and once again had brought them back to this same promised land. How good God was to the Israel of Moses' and Joshua's day, and how good God had been to them also.

Finally, we note once again the prominence of the reading of the law of the Lord. Nehemiah 8:18 records, "Ezra read out of the book of the law of God every day, from the first day to the last. The Israelites celebrated the feast for seven days, and on the eighth day there was an assembly, according to the ordinance." God had granted His people such a heart to know and obey His word, and we can only long for the Lord to shower this same grace and favor on us.

Learning Activity

Thinking Back

Think of a time when each of the following had a spiritual impact on your life. Jot down a few words to remind you of when and where that took place and how you responded.

1. Listening to the public reading of God's Word —

2. Hearing someone explain a passage of Scripture —

3. Realizing personal failure in applying a specific biblical teaching —

4. Gathering with a large group for a religious celebration —

For Your Consideration

1. For those in positions of leadership, including fathers, elders, and deacons—do you see from Scripture indication that it is more important for you to learn God's Word? If so, where is this indicated? What would happen in the families of your church, and in your church as a whole, if leaders took more seriously their added responsibility to learn the Word of God?

2. Are you as willing to quickly and promptly obey God's Word as the people in Nehemiah's day were? What would help us be ready to hear and obey whatever God teaches us to do? How can we better have hearts eager to follow His ways?

Renewing the Covenant Community

Bible Truth: *Confessing sin, praising God, and continuous obedience are evidences of genuine renewal in God's people.*

Life Impact: *To help you pursue the renewal of God's people, beginning with personal renewal*

Confession and Praise (Neh. 9:1-37)

Have you even considered how important history is to God? From reading the Bible we see clearly that the history of God's people—how they lived, whether they obeyed Him or not, what His commandments were to them and how they responded, His judgment or punishment of their rebellion, His merciful forgiveness of their sin, the record of His blessing and His gracious promise and favor—has high value in God's sight. Just think for a moment how much of the Bible records history for us. Whole books and sections of Scripture, in both Old and New Testaments, are made up of the historical records of how God revealed Himself to His people, how they lived before Him, and how He worked with them in their times of obedience and disobedience. History matters!

A CLOSER LOOK

Showing Humility

As the people of Israel prepared for their national confession of sin, they fasted, wore sackcloth, and put dust on their heads (Neh. 9:1). All three of those actions were external expressions of their humility before God.

The *Holman Bible Dictionary* defines humility as "a personal quality in which an individual shows dependence on God and respect for other persons."[1] This requires (1) an awareness of the contrast between our sinfulness and God's holiness, (2) a willingness to submit ourselves to God and His authority, and (3) a recognition that other people are valuable to God. Those inward qualities signal the sincere humility God desires from us, and He is much more interested in those signs than our external expressions that may or may not be sincere (Isa. 58:3-7).

Subjecting our desires to the wishes of God and the well-being of others is an important aspect of the Christian life and the very picture of Christlikeness. Paul said in Philippians 2:3-8, "Do nothing out of rivalry or conceit, but in humility consider others as more important than yourselves. Everyone should look out not only for his own interests, but also for the interests of others. Make your own attitude that of Christ Jesus, who, existing in the form of God . . . humbled Himself."

---

1. See Gary Hardin, "Humility" in *Holman Bible Dictionary*, Trent Butler, gen. ed. (Nashville: Holman Bible Publishers, 1991), 676.

Israel's History

When the Levites stood up, they started singing Israel's song. Look at Nehemiah 9:5-37 and outline the key points in Israel's religious history. Fill in the blanks.

1. God c_____ Israel (9:5-6).

2. God c_____ Israel (9:7).

3. God made a c_____ with Israel (9:8).

4. God heard the c_____ of Israel (9:9).

5. God r_____ Israel from Egyptian slavery (9:10-11).

6. God l_____ Israel in the wilderness (9:12).

7. God gave the S_____ and the l_____ to Israel (9:12-14).

8. God p_____ for Israel (9:15).

9. Israel r_____ against God (9:16-18).

10. God g_____ and cared for Israel anyway (9:19-21).

11. God gave Israel the promised l_____ (9:22-25).

12, Israel r_____ against God (9:26).

13. God handed Israel over to her e_____ (9:27).

14. Israel c_____ out to God (9:27).

15. God r_____ Israel (9:27).

16. Israel r_____ against God (9:28-29).

17. God was p_____ with Israel (9:30-31).

18. Israel now confessed its w_____ and God's f_____ (9:32-37).

And in particular God wants us to learn from the history of His relationship with His people, the Israelites.

Nehemiah 9 largely retells the history of God's people. The record of God's relationship with Israel is presented in a sweeping overview, and the rehearsing of this history elicits from God's people deep repentance before Him. Why does God care so much about the history of His dealings with His people, and what can we learn from it?

As Nehemiah 9 begins, the joyous Feast of Booths had concluded, and the people resumed their posture of repentance before the Lord. When Ezra and the Levites read the law of Moses to the people early in the seventh month, the people responded with mourning and weeping over their disobedience to the very law of God they had just heard about.

Because Israel was commanded to celebrate the joyous Feast of Booths at the beginning of the seventh month, the people were commanded not to weep but rather to rejoice (8:9-12). On the eighth day, however, the feast culminated with a solemn assembly of worship, and the law of Moses was read again in their hearing.

When God's Word is read at some length and when God's people listen attentively and receptively to what God has revealed, a deep sense of contrition before the Lord is often the result. This is exactly what happened to the people of Israel. On the 24th day of this same 7th month, the Israelites assembled, fasting and wearing sackcloth with dust on their heads (9:1)—all three symbols of their humility before God, in recognition of their sin and desperate need. Furthermore, they had learned from the law that they were not to marry people from other nations and ethnic groups. So they came together as the people whom God had chosen and confessed their sin and the sin of those Israelites before them who had so grievously violated the law of the Lord (v. 2).

Remarkably, we also read that "while they stood in their places, they read from the book of the law of the LORD their God for a fourth of the day and spent another fourth of the day in confession and worship of the LORD their God" (v. 3). The intensity of longing to hear and learn from God's law continued in Israel, and this led to sustained times of confession of sin and honoring the very God whose word they had broken in the past.

To stimulate the people's recommitment to the Lord, the Levites who read the law to the people now were led to recite highlights of the history of God's relationship with Israel. And what a history this was! Reading Nehemiah 9:5-31 provides a rich overview of God's greatness, glory, grace, and mercy, along with Israel's very checkered relationship with God. While we cannot look at every detail of this well-crafted survey of Israel's history, we can notice some of the key elements.

First, the greatness, uniqueness, supremacy, and glory of God began this historical overview, and this theme set the stage for all else that followed. As the Levites addressed the people, they cried out, "Bless the LORD your God from everlasting to everlasting. Praise Your glorious name, and may it be exalted above all blessing and praise. You alone are the LORD. You created the heavens, the highest heavens with all their host, the earth and all that is on it, the seas and all that are in them. You give life to all of them and the heavenly host worships You" (vv. 5b-6). As with many such portions of Scripture extolling the greatness of God, these verses not only declare that God, as Creator, is supreme over all His creation. They also declare God's rightful ownership and rulership of His people. Reminding God's people that God is Creator of all underscores His rightful ownership of all.

The Bible wants us to understand this principle: To create is to own, and to own is to have absolute rights of rulership. Even before we read of God's choice of Israel as His people, we should already conclude that God has absolute rights over them by virtue of His being their Creator, along with everything that exits. God alone is God. And God alone is Creator of all that exists. We are to acknowledge that He alone is rightful Lord and we owe everything to Him.

Second, this God who has absolute rights over heaven and earth as sole Creator is the same God who has shown such favor and attentive care to Israel. This began when God chose a man from Ur of the Chaldeans, Abram, and changed his name to Abraham (meaning "father of a multitude"). Fully apart from any merit in Abram, God chose this one man through whom He would form His people (who would become the people of Israel). To his descendants God would give the land of the Canaanites as their permanent land (vv. 7-8). Since the people of Israel in the time of Nehemiah had just recently returned to this land, the Levites reminded them that from the beginning God's plan was that this land would belong to them and their descendants. Their present return to the land, though they remained in distress, showed that God was in the process of keeping His promise, for He is righteous in all His ways (v. 8b).

Not only was God's favor shown them through choosing Abram and giving his descendants a land, but God also showed favor to them by redeeming them from bondage in Egypt in a miraculous deliverance. Although their lives were threatened as they left Egypt, God opened up the sea for them to cross on dry ground and He brought all of their pursuers to ruin (vv. 9-11). God not only created these people and chose them as His own, but He also redeemed them from bondage so they would be His own people.

God's favor expanded as God gave to these blessed people His "impartial ordinances, reliable instructions, and good decrees and commandments" (v. 13) through Moses on Mount Sinai. In the law of the Lord, God showed His people how they might be rightly related to Him and live lives of the greatest blessing and joy. During their wilderness testing, God provided both food and drink so they could learn that the God who demanded unrestricted obedience from them was the same God who loved and cared them. They received both God's good law and God's kind provision and protection. How blessed and favored Israel had been.

Third, despite God's creation and calling of Israel to be His people and despite the extraordinary favor and blessing He bestowed on them, over and again Israel rebelled against God. The Levites, speaking publicly to the Lord, reminded the people that their "ancestors acted arrogantly; they became stiff-necked and did not listen to Your commands. They refused to listen and did not remember Your wonders You performed among them" (vv. 16-17a). Both here and again later in this chapter, the Levites reminded the Israelites just how sinful they had been, even in the face of such kindness and goodness from the Lord's hand. In the second reminder of Israel's rebellion, the Levites rehearsed how their fathers "were disobedient and rebelled against You. They flung Your law behind their backs and killed Your prophets who warned them to turn them back to You. They committed terrible blasphemies" (v. 26).

Fourth, for such flagrant rebellion, Israel deserved only God's punishment and wrath. To turn from the one true God who is full of both glory and goodness calls forth divine judgment. God, therefore, brought His heavy hand of discipline on His people. The form of the punishment was fitted to God's promised blessing. God had promised that as they obeyed Him they would live in the land and God would prosper them. But in their disobedience, God judged them by giving them into the hands of foreign oppressors who took them into exile (vv. 27,30b). This might seem the end of the story. Surely for such grievous offenses and transgressions, God would now abandon His people once and for all.

But last, God's final word to His people was not one of judgment but of renewal and restored blessing. Marvel at God's compassion as He heard the agonizing cry of His people even in their rebellion. He had promised never to forsake them utterly but would bring them back into their land (as was happening in Nehemiah's day). As the Levites concluded this rehearsal of Israel's checkered history, to God they said, "In Your abundant compassion, You did not destroy them or abandon them, for You are a gracious and compassionate God" (v. 31). And as they summarized the meaning of this history for their lives as God's people, they could not have been more accurate than when they said to the Lord, "You are righteous concerning all that has come on us, because You have acted faithfully, while we have acted wickedly" (v. 33). Because of this wickedness and sin, even though God has shown mercy in bringing them back to their land, yet they were still living in distress in this land of promise (v. 27). God's full blessing had not been restored to its promised fullness, and so the Levites called out to God to hear again the cry of their hearts for His mercy to be shown (v. 32).

Surely, Israel's sin throughout its history has been great. But God's mercy has always been greater. So here, the Levites called on Israel to fall before God, confess their sin, and renew their commitment to Him alone.

For Your Consideration

1. Since God gives us so much history in the Bible, He must want us to learn from it. What are some of the main lessons for your life that you can take away from this historical account in Nehemiah 9?

2. Why do you think the Israelites turned away from the Lord, again and again, despite the great favor He showed to them? What is it about them (and us) that would lead to such sin and rebellion?

3. When you read about God's forgiving the sin of those who have rebelled against Him, how do you respond? Is forgiveness from God an entitlement that His people should expect? Is the grace of God shown to Israel, and to us, truly amazing? When this is not the case, what has gone wrong with how we think about God and His grace?

Renewed Commitments
(Neh. 9:38–10:39)

In light of such great divine mercy in the face of widespread sin, Nehemiah called on the people of Israel to make a renewed commitment to the Lord. As recorded in Nehemiah 9:38, the leaders throughout Israel came together to pledge their obedience: "In view of all this," the Levites declared, "we are making a binding agreement in writing on a sealed document containing the names of our leaders, Levites, and priests." Following this, a list of names is given, some of which we've seen before as those singled out to stand with Ezra in his reading of the law. But many other names also appear. Even though we do not know most of these people, the point of listing their names is clear: God's gracious work among His people had resulted in widespread revival. All of the Israelites had united with one heart and mind to sign their names to an agreement pledging their renewed obedience to God alone. This was a red-letter day in the history of a largely disobedient people. God's grace had brought them back to their land, and God's grace was at work renewing their hearts. Even though this pledge of obedience did not prevent ongoing sin from taking place (see chap. 13), and even though the fullness of Israel's restoration still waited some future work of God (see Rom. 11:25-26), still this pledge of renewed obedience to God was a clear evidence God had once again been faithful to His people. He had not abandoned them utterly. He had shown them great mercy. Here we see a small anticipation of the coming day when all of God's people will pledge their obedience to Him and they (we) will all fulfill it!

The actual obligations the people agreed to in writing involved some of the most important aspects of keeping the law of Moses. For example, the Israelites signing this agreement pledged not to "give our daughters in marriage to the surrounding peoples and will not take their daughters as wives for our sons" (Neh. 10:30). Through Moses, prior to the conquest of the promised land, God commanded Israel not to intermarry with the peoples of the land of Canaan. To do so, God said, would result in their turning to other gods (for example, Ex. 34:11-17; Deut. 7:1-6). And since intermarriage had been a particularly difficult issue when the people were in exile, they pledged that they would not allow intermarriage to continue.

The Israelites also agreed to be diligent in keeping the Sabbath as a day of worship to the Lord. As a sign of their trust in God's provision, they promised to bring the firstfruits of their produce, as the law required, in recognition that God was their provider and their strength. Significantly, they also pledged to bring the firstborn of their houses, herds, and flocks to the Lord. And they pledged to tithe and to give generously to support the work of the priests and Levites. The chapter ends with a sober and God-honoring pledge, "We will not neglect the house of our God" (Neh. 10:39).

We would do well to reflect on how this marvelous account of God's grace and the people's recommitment can apply to our lives today. First, the law's requirement that the people not intermarry was given, at its root, because God desired His people to be holy. The holiness of God's people meant that they were to be set apart to God, different from the world—like God in His moral character and not like the world and its ways.

Throughout the Bible God calls His people to embrace the call to holiness. This call requires us not to join ourselves to people and practices contrary to God's will and ways. We must care more about what God thinks than what others think. We must accept our call to be different from those in the world, even when our holiness appears to them foolish or offensive. This pledge of recommitment in Nehemiah 10 was a pledge to holiness, and this is where every pledge to God must begin. Any other pledge to God will be sheer hypocrisy if we do not offer to God our sincere commitment to live consistently as His holy people.

Second, several other aspects of the written agreement made by the people involved their resources and money. They pledged to tithe—to give the firstfruits of their crops, to offer the firstborn of their children, herds, and flocks, and generously to support the priests and Levites. Not surprisingly, what comes to the top of

the list when considering the obedience God requires of us is also our use of the money and other resources He provides for us. One theme emphasized throughout the history of Israel given by the Levites (9:5-31) was how faithful God had been in providing for His people. God cares for His own, and He is faithful to those who trust in Him. His faithfulness is manifest, in part, by His provision and protection. The only right response to such lavish care is to place our trust in God, not in money and things. Perhaps this is why Jesus said we cannot love both God and money (Matt. 6:24). Money functions as a substitute god; it competes for our trust, our hope, our devotion, and our love. Therefore, one clear mark of true revival, of true commitment to God alone, is when people's hearts are freed to trust God and use their money in ways that obey God and advance His kingdom. Put simply, true commitment to God involves a freedom to give.

Dan Klepper

Third, their recommitment to God also involved a commitment to worship. The Sabbath Day was reserved as a day of worship, a time devoted to learning from God's Word and adoring God's name. Another mark of true revival is seen when God's people love to meet together for such learning and adoration. May we today be blessed by God's grace as the Israelites of old were. May we likewise be marked by such holiness of life, freedom of giving, and longing for worship. May revival come to us as it did to them.

For Your Consideration

1. What is your attitude toward holiness? Do you respond positively to what holiness is? Is it your heart's longing to be holy? If the truth were known about your life, how would you measure up to God's call for you to be holy?

2. How do you respond to calls to give of your resources and money? What is the relationship between having a heart that trusts God and being free to give generously?

3. Do you love the worship of God? Do you long to hear His voice and learn His Word? Does your heart rejoice at offering to Him your praise? How may we in our churches enlarge our love of true worship?

Learning Activity

Analyzing the Vow

What was the significance of each part of the Israelites' vow? What would be appropriate commitments for us to make in each of these four areas? (Choose your answers for the first two columns from the lists below.)

	VOW What did the Israelites promise to do or not do?	AREA To what area of godly living did that vow relate?	APPLICATION What commitment might I make to enhance that area of godly living in myself?
10:29			
10:30			
10:31			
10:32-39			

ANSWERS: Vows: Follow the law of God; Avoid intermarriage with pagan people; Observe the Sabbath; Provide materially for the religious leaders and the House of God **Areas:** Obedience; Holiness; Devotion; Faith

Willing and
Determined to Serve

Bible Truth: *Opportunities to serve God abound, and all of God's people are to seek ways they can serve.*

Life Impact: *To help you serve God willingly in all the opportunities He gives you*

Service Through Relocation (Neh. 11:1-18)

With the temple restored under Ezra's leadership (Ezra 6:13-18) and with the gates and wall of Jerusalem rebuilt under Nehemiah's leadership (Neh. 6:15-19), the time had come to put the city of Jerusalem on a more stable footing. Obviously, all of the commitment, courage, and hard work that had gone into bringing Jerusalem back from ruins would have been lost if the faithful Israelites had all returned to their homes throughout Judea. Jerusalem needed its own permanent citizens to maintain the city and to protect it against possible future assault. But who would stay?

Before we look at the answer Nehemiah 11 gives to this question, let's consider why this was even an issue. Wouldn't all of the people who helped rebuild Jerusalem's wall want to stay and live in this grand city of

A CLOSER LOOK

Music in Worship

When Nehemiah led the Israelites to dedicate the wall in a time of worship of God, he planned for music to be included in the event. There was "singing accompanied by cymbals, harps, and lyres" (Neh. 12:27). The singers Nehemiah used were a standing group of temple workers, along with the priests, Levites, gatekeepers, and servants (Ezra 2:70).

Music is mentioned often in the Bible in connection with individual and corporate worship. The Book of Psalms contains many first-person songs. For instance, "I will sing to the Lord because He has treated me graciously," David said in Psalm 13:6. Psalm 30:4 says, "Sing to the Lord, you His faithful ones, and praise His holy name"—songs intended for the whole community to sing together in worship.

The New Testament calls for Christians to speak "to one another in psalms, hymns, and spiritual songs, singing and making music to the Lord in your heart" (Eph. 5:19).

Christian music has changed through the years. Even the most traditional Baptist churches rarely sing music more than a few hundred years old. Some use only Christian songs written in the past few decades. Most Baptist churches use a mixture of the old and the new.

Musical instruments used in worship have also changed through the centuries. When the organ was first invented, many objected to its use in worship. Some today object to the use of guitars and drums in worship, but those instruments are actually from the same musical families as the cymbals, harps, and lyres used at the dedication of the wall of Jerusalem.

The important thing to remember is that music is intended to be an aid to our worship of God. It should not distract us from worship, but should enhance our worship. The real test is not what kind of music we use, or whether we use music at all. The real test is whether we worship God in spirit and in truth (John 4:24).

God? Wouldn't the problem be finding those who would be willing to live elsewhere, since too many would want to live in the city itself? Interestingly, this was not the case.

Probably at least two reasons were primary for why more people would want to live elsewhere than in Jerusalem itself. First, many of the people who moved temporarily to Jerusalem in response to the call to rebuild its walls owned their own homes and lands in surrounding towns. As happy as they would be that Jerusalem had been restored, they would love for other people to live there so they could return to their homes. Second, Jerusalem had always been a dangerous place to live—not because of the large number of robbers and murderers living there (as is the case in our modern-day cities)—but rather, because Jerusalem was a target for those who despised the God of Israel and who wanted to bring the Jews to ruin. To live in Jerusalem required accepting the possibility of enemy attack and standing ready to defend the city even at the cost of one's own life, property, and family. Great risks awaited the future inhabitants of Jerusalem. Some equitable means had to be found to determine who would live there and who would return to their homes elsewhere.

The decision was that the leaders who had directed the rebuilding of the wall and inspired the people to trust God through much opposition would live in Jerusalem. For them, this was one of the great triumphs of their lives, and it was natural that they remain. For the rest of the people, however, they "cast lots for one out of ten to come and live in Jerusalem, the holy city, while the other nine-tenths remained in their towns. The people praised all the men who volunteered to live in Jerusalem" (Neh. 11:1-2). What courage this took, and what commitment to see Jerusalem's safety and prosperity secured by their willingness to live in and defend "the holy city" of God.

One wonders just why the proportion of "one out of ten" was used for deciding the number of the inhabitants of the city. No doubt, simple pragmatic interests were considered—the overall size of the city and roughly how many could comfortably live within its walls. But possibly, an earlier reference to the plan God gave to Nehemiah even before the walls were rebuilt was coming to fruition. Recall Nehemiah's comment that "my God put it into my mind to assemble the nobles, the officials, and the people to be registered by genealogy" (7:5). Perhaps Nehemiah at last was seeing the culmination of the vision God had given him originally of the city both rebuilt and teeming with new residents. In any case, the presence of these citizens was further evidence of God's gracious provision and work to restore blessing to Jerusalem.

Although this chapter is tedious to read, one must remember that without citizens living in the city, the whole project of the restoration of Jerusalem would have been for naught. Seen this way, Nehemiah 11 records God's grace and favor to move the hearts of so many to accept the difficult and potentially dangerous challenge of moving within the walls of the grand city. That God will not fail in fulfilling what He had promised is seen in the listing of names in this chapter. Surely more awaited to be done before the full realization of God's promises were completed. But this truly was a great milestone in the unfolding of the fulfillment of God's promised blessing to His people.

For Your Consideration

1. Put yourself in the place of an Israelite who owned land and a home in some Judean town, not in Jerusalem. Imagine what you would feel if the lot fell to you. What would your values and commitments need to be for you to accept this call to relocate and live in the city of Jerusalem?

2. Have you ever considered whether God might want you to relocate? After all, it should be clear to us that this is His right—altogether! Since God has full ownership of our lives, how open are we to living wherever He calls us to live, doing whatever He directs us to do?

3. Should only some Christian people seriously consider the possibility that God might call them to be missionaries? Does it not stand to reason that God wants everyone to be willing to go, even if only "one out of ten" are chosen?

Service Through Celebration
(Neh. 12:27-43)

As the writer of Ecclesiastes said, there is "a time to weep and a time to laugh; a time to mourn and a time to dance" (Eccl. 3:4). And in Jerusalem, the weeping and mourning were past, and the time for laughter, dancing, and celebration had come!

I imagine there has seldom been such singing, celebration, worship, and joy in any gathering, in all of human history, as there was among the faithful in Israel at the dedication of the restored wall of Jerusalem. The Levites were sought out to provide hymns of thanksgiving and songs of joy, accompanied by choirs and numerous instruments. Musical leaders were chosen with care, and the numbers and kinds of instruments were selected to enhance the tone of celebration and praise. Two great choirs were appointed, each given specific instructions for where they should stand and sing and just when and how each should participate. The priests got ready their sacrifices to bring before the Lord, and the officials of Jerusalem, with Nehemiah, gathered in the house of God. Enormous planning and synchronizing went into a service meant to express before the Lord the joy and thanksgiving that filled their hearts. When finally the singing and celebration and sacrifices commenced, Nehemiah described some of what it was like: "The two thanksgiving processions stood in the house of God. So did I and half of the officials accompanying me, as well as the priests:…Then the singers sang, with Jezrahiah as the leader. On that day they offered great sacrifices and rejoiced because God had given them great joy. The women and children also celebrated, and Jerusalem's rejoicing was heard far away" (Neh. 12:40-43).

We should recognize that the Lord was responsible for giving the people the courage and the will to rebuild Jerusalem's wall amidst great opposition. God moved their hearts to recommit themselves to Him and to keeping His law. And just as surely, God is to be credited for making their celebration sweet and joyful. As Nehemiah put it, the people rejoiced "because God had given them great joy" (v. 43). From beginning to end, God was at work to bring about the return of His people to

At the dedication of the wall, they celebrated with "singing accompanied by cymbals, harps, and lyres" (Neh. 12:27).

Illustrator Photos/David Rogers/British Museum

Jerusalem. God worked in them to accomplish the vision He put into Nehemiah's heart. And God continued His work in them by granting them true joy in their dedication of the wall. So once again, may God be glorified because He has done great things!

One more item should be noted. Not only did the people rejoice greatly at the dedication of the wall, but they also gave all that was required of them to the singers, priests, Levites, and gatekeepers for the service these key people rendered on that day of celebration (vv. 44-47). As Nehemiah commented, "The legally required portions for the priests and Levites were gathered from the village fields, because Judah was grateful to the priests and Levites who were serving" (v. 44). The people's gratitude for the services being rendered led them to give freely to meet the needs of those who made it possible. Great joy and great giving go together. When God is at work inciting joy, He also will be at work inspiring His people to give.

For Your Consideration

1. Do you sometimes wonder whether planning should be done for worship services to be honoring to the Lord? Have you ever heard the sentiment that we should "just let the Spirit move" and not worry about planning? What can we learn on this issue from this account?

Learning Activity

Multiple Choice

Check the answer or answers you think are best for each of the following questions.

1. Why didn't all the Jews settle in Jerusalem?
   ___ A. There wasn't room for all of them in the city.
   ___ B. Some people just preferred the suburbs.
   ___ C. Most of the workers already had their own homes elsewhere.
   ___ D. Jerusalem was a risky place to live, being a primary target of their enemies.

2. Who was selected to stay in Jerusalem?
   ___ A. Everyone under 20 and over 60.
   ___ B. Women and children.
   ___ C. Leaders and one-tenth of the others, chosen by lot.
   ___ D. Only those with pure blood and no intermarriage.

3. Why did so many help rebuild Jerusalem if they had no desire to live there?
   ___ A. They were paid well for their labor.
   ___ B. Rebuilding the wall was a matter of ethnic and national pride.
   ___ C. They needed a national and religious center.
   ___ D. They did it to honor God.

4. If God called me to leave home and relocate to another place, I would
   ___ A. Assume I had misunderstood God.
   ___ B. Start packing.
   ___ C. Do it, but hate it.
   ___ D. Ignore the call.

2. How well do we do in our churches in celebrating the victories that God grants to us? What can we learn about this dedication service that would help free us to worship the Lord with joy?

3. What is the connection between gratitude toward God and giving to the work of God? Given this connection, would it stand to reason that if we wish for giving to increase, we should ask God to increase our level of gratitude? Explain your response. How can we cultivate in our lives and churches a stronger sense of genuine gratitude before God?

Service Through Vigilant Leadership (Neh. 13:6-31)

After all that happened through the Book of Nehemiah, one would not expect it to end this way. The last chapter of this great book records four significant areas of sin and disregard for the law of the Lord that continued in Jerusalem, even after all God had done, and even after the vows of recommitment written and signed by all the leaders of the city. Perhaps this is a way of God reminding us that no revival on this earth, no matter how amazing and widespread, will produce an end of sin or of sinful tendencies among God's people—not, that is, until the Lord returns. Despite God's gracious work, we remain "prone to wander" as the song writer put it, "prone to leave the God I love."[1] Such continues to be the case with Israel, and it is on this note that the book ends.

Nehemiah was forced to confront four specific areas where the law of God was being disregarded. First, they had read in the law that no Ammonite or Moabite was to enter the house of the Lord (note: Ammon and Moab were the two countries, directly opposite the heart of the land of Israel, just east of the Jordan River).

The reason the law commanded this was simple: these two nations opposed the children of Israel during the days of their wilderness wanderings, even hiring Balaam to curse Israel, though God turned the curse into a blessing (Neh. 13:1-2). In response to reading this in the law of the Lord (from Deut. 23:3-5), the Israelites excluded the foreigners (Ammonites and Edomites) from Israel (Neh. 13:3). But despite this clear teaching from the law, Eliashib the priest had allowed Tobiah the Ammonite to remain in Israel, even preparing a room for him to stay inside the house of God (v. 7). Nehemiah had been out of the country when Eliashib made these arrangements. When Nehemiah returned and learned of this, he was horrified. After all, Tobiah not only was an Ammonite but he also was one of the greatest enemies of Israel in rebuilding the wall (2:10). He and Sanballat had lead the opposition from the beginning. Knowing that God's law was being violated, Nehemiah did what he had to do: he removed Tobiah and all of his goods from the house of God, cleansed the room where Tobiah stayed, and returned the utensils to their proper places (13:7-9).

Second, Nehemiah discovered that the Levites and singers were not being given the portions owed to them. Knowing that this also violated the law of God, he appointed certain qualified men to oversee the distribution of the portions to those to whom the payments were required (vv. 11-13). Nehemiah's leadership and courage were once again exercised in not only addressing a problem but in finding a solution that would avoid ongoing violations of the law.

Third, Nehemiah became aware that some were working at their winepresses and hauling their grain on the Sabbath. He confronted these people, asking them why they did such evil, "profaning the Sabbath day" (v. 17). He reminded them that for such sins God's heavy hand of discipline had fallen on Israel in the past. He warned them that profaning the Sabbath would invite God's wrath. But Nehemiah did not stop here. He also commanded that guards be stationed at the gates of Jerusalem to ensure that no workers would be able to enter or leave the city on the Sabbath. Because of the seriousness of this sin in God's sight, Nehemiah determined that he should do everything he could to ensure the Sabbath was kept holy to the Lord.

Finally, Nehemiah became aware that some of the Jews had married women from foreign nations and that their children were actually being raised speaking the languages of those other countries (vv. 23-24). Rather than create even greater disruption to life by requiring these Jews to divorce their foreign wives, Nehemiah commanded them not to give their sons or daughters to foreigners. Again he reminded them of how many of Solomon's problems came when he brought to himself foreign wives—how even this godly king was led to act unfaithfully against God by marrying foreign women.

In all these ways, Nehemiah exhibited faithfulness to God and His law, and he showed great courage and wisdom in his leadership over the people. Though this last chapter reminds us that sin will remain a vivid reality for the people of God until our Lord returns, we also see the difference godly leadership can make. May God give to His church such men of faithfulness, courage, and wisdom, and may His church grow in purity and holiness to His glory and honor.

Learning Activity

Vows Made, Broken, and Renewed

The first column lists vows made by the Israelites that you studied in the previous lesson. In the second column, list verses from Nehemiah 13 that show the people failed to keep the vows. In the third column, summarize what Nehemiah did to put the people back on track in keeping their original vows.

VOWS MADE	VOWS BROKEN	VOWS RENEWED
10:29–To follow the law of God	Nehemiah 13: ___	
10:30–To avoid intermarriage with pagan people	Nehemiah 13: ___	
10:31–To observe the Sabbath	Nehemiah 13: ___	
10:32-39–To provide materially for the religious leaders and the house of God	Nehemiah 13: ___	

ANSWERS:

Vows broken	Vows renewed
Neh. 13:8-9	Threw Tobiah the Ammonite out of the house of God
Neh. 13:23-31	Rebuked those guilty and required an oath that they would not give their children in marriage to pagan peoples
Neh. 13:15-22	Rebuked the people for buying and selling on the Sabbath and ordered the gates closed
Neh. 13:10-14	Called back religious leaders and appointed treasurers to receive and disburse funds

For Your Consideration

1. What are the main qualities of leadership you admire in Nehemiah? How can we grow in ways that would enable us to respond to hard situations more as he did?

2. Do you find it discouraging that the Book of Nehemiah ends the way it does? What is God wanting to teach us by putting on display the ongoing temptations and sins of His people, even after such marvelous victories?

---

1. "Come Thou Fount of Every Blessing," No. 15, *The Baptist Hymnal,* 1991.

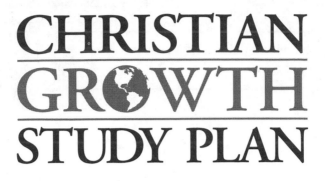

CHRISTIAN GROWTH STUDY PLAN

In the **Christian Growth Study Plan (formerly Church Study Course),** this book, *Serving God with Determined Faith: Studies in the Book of Nehemiah,* is a resource for course credit in the subject area Leadership and Skill Development of the Christian Growth category of plans. To receive credit, read the book, complete the learning activities, show your work to your pastor, a staff member or church leader, then complete the following information. This page may be duplicated. Send the completed page to: **Christian Growth Study Plan • One LifeWay Plaza • Nashville, TN 37234-0117 • FAX: (615)251-5067 • Email:** *cgspnet@lifeway.com.*

For information about the Christian Growth Study Plan, refer to the Christian Growth Study Plan Catalog. It is located online at *www.lifeway.com/cgsp.* If you do not have access to the Internet, contact the Christian Growth Study Plan office (1.800.968.5519) for the specific plan you need for your ministry.

Serving God with Determined Faith: Studies in the Book of Nehemiah
COURSE NUMBER: CG-1123

PARTICIPANT INFORMATION

Social Security Number (USA ONLY-optional)   –   –

Personal CGSP Number*   –   –

Date of Birth (MONTH, DAY, YEAR)   –   –

Name (First, Middle, Last)

Home Phone   –   –

Address (Street, Route, or P.O. Box)

City, State, or Province

Zip/Postal Code

Please check appropriate box: ❑ Resource purchased by self ❑ Resource purchased by church ❑ Other

CHURCH INFORMATION

Church Name

Address (Street, Route, or P.O. Box)

City, State, or Province

Zip/Postal Code

CHANGE REQUEST ONLY

☐ Former Name

☐ Former Address

City, State, or Province

Zip/Postal Code

☐ Former Church

City, State, or Province

Zip/Postal Code

Signature of Pastor, Conference Leader, or Other Church Leader

Date

*New participants are requested but not required to give SS# and date of birth. Existing participants, please give CGSP# when using SS# for the first time. Thereafter, only one ID# is required. **Mail to:** Christian Growth Study Plan, One LifeWay Plaza, Nashville, TN 37234-0117. Fax: (615)251-5067.

Rev. 3-03